Educational Theory in British Children's Literary Classics

Education and Popular Culture

Series Editors: Ludovic A. Sourdot (Texas Woman's University) and Edward Janak (University of Toledo)

Education and Popular Culture provides a place for teachers and scholars to explore ways in which popular culture has been utilized for research and teaching purposes. The series editors believe that popular culture allows people to connect in meaningful ways and make sense of the world in which we live. The series is unique as it equally values practitioner-generated pieces on using mass/popular culture as it does theoretician-oriented pieces on studying mass/popular culture, as well as works that exist in the intersections between these worlds. Works in this series take up issues surrounding popular culture in education broadly through pedagogical, historical, sociological, and critical lenses.

Books in Series

Educational Theory in British Children's Literary Classics: Teaching and Learning Down the Rabbit Hole, by Thomas Albritton

Unlearning the Gender Binary with Trans Masculine YouTube Vloggers: Reframing Sex, by Stevie N. Berberick

Education and the Female Superhero: Slayers, Cyborgs, Sorority Sisters, and Schoolteachers, by Andrew Grunzke

Educational Theory in British Children's Literary Classics

Teaching and Learning Down the Rabbit Hole

Thomas Albritton

LEXINGTON BOOKS

Lanham • Boulder • New York • London

Published by Lexington Books
An imprint of The Rowman & Littlefield Publishing Group, Inc.
4501 Forbes Boulevard, Suite 200, Lanham, Maryland 20706
www.rowman.com

6 Tinworth Street, London SE11 5AL, United Kingdom

British Library Cataloguing in Publication Information Available

Library of Congress Cataloging-in-Publication Data

Names: Albritton, Thomas, 1959- author.
Title: Educational theory in British children's literary classics : teaching and learning
    down the rabbit hole / Thomas Albritton.
Description: Lanham : Lexington Books, 2021. | Series: Education and popular culture |
    Includes bibliographical references and index.
Identifiers: LCCN 2021014935 (print) | LCCN 2021014936 (ebook) |
    ISBN 9781793616319 (cloth) | ISBN 9781793616326 (epub)
Subjects: LCSH: Children's literature, English—History and criticism. |
    Education in literature.
Classification: LCC PR990 .A43 2021 (print) | LCC PR990 (ebook) |
    DDC 823.009/3557083—dc23
LC record available at https://lccn.loc.gov/2021014935
LC ebook record available at https://lccn.loc.gov/2021014936

♾™ The paper used in this publication meets the minimum requirements of American
National Standard for Information Sciences—Permanence of Paper for Printed Library
Materials, ANSI/NISO Z39.48-1992.

To my late parents, Thomas W. Albritton, Sr., and Norma Ruth Kelly Albritton, who understood very few things, ever, about my educational dreams and pursuits, but who never wavered in their support of them.

Contents

Foreword by the Series Editors

Thomas Albritton looks at things in incredibly unique ways. And that is fortunate for us.

He is a "frequent flier" at the Popular Culture Association's annual national meeting. His presentations are intellectually engaging, highly creative, often humorous, and always unique. In fact, when we were pitching the idea of this series to Lexington Books, Dr. Albritton was one of the potential contributors we had in mind when describing the purpose of the series: to provide an outlet to scholars who look at things in different ways. We are grateful to the readers of this volume, and sincerely hope you enjoy the author's perspective; we complimentarily describe it as rarefied thinking and mean that with sincerity, not irony. The author states this work is neither literary scholarship nor educational scholarship but situated someplace in between. To that end, this volume is something extremely rare: an author's original voice filtered primarily through his own insights, and those of his students past and present.

In today's media saturated age (Social media! Golden age of television! Satellite radio! Streaming music! Peak TV! Podcasts! YouTube!) it is easy to forget that literature has been, and continues to be, a form of mass culture and entertainment. If we define mass culture as any media designed to be consumed by the dominant culture, and mass media as a means of communicating ideas to a broad audience, children's literature easily fits both definitions. Not many would disagree in the ubiquity of *Alice in Wonderland*; it does us well to remember the near-mania that accompanied the release of the last volumes in the Harry Potter series. By some estimates, there have been over half a billion Harry Potter books sold—meaning that one out of every fifteen people *on the planet* owns at least one volume set in Hogwarts.

The lessons shared in this volume are valuable to teachers on all levels. The author states he hopes "the journey through these essays animates your imagination, enriches your conversation, and expands your alertness for educational insight." We believe it has the potential to do all the above. The author's arguments are logical and cogent and take the reader in new directions that are likely not to have occurred before. We hope that you, as a reader, pause as frequently and often as we do, as listeners and editors, to say "wow, I never thought of it like that before!"

While focusing on British children's literature, this book presents a substantive critique of the culture of schooling in the US, particularly in the neoliberal era in which we live. Alice unsuccessfully tries to resolve the challenges she faces by recounting context-less lessons from her schooling (and those overheard from her older siblings); Peter Rabbit's exploits show the shortcomings in formalistic education; Captain Hook can be read as a "good Eton boy" and thus becomes exhibit A in how traditional schooling fails students; the adventures of Rat and Mole reflect the echoes and shadows in Plato's Allegory of the Cave; and beyond the obvious messianic narrative, the conflict between Aslan and the White Witch can be read as authentic vs. inauthentic (but high stakes) assessment. This critique becomes all the clearer in the books' final two chapters, which focus specifically on how learners come to knowledge (via a Hobbit) and the act of teaching in the culture of schooling (via Hogwarts).

And, with that said, we welcome you to join us and the author as we duck down the rabbit hole together.

Acknowledgments

I would like to begin by thanking Ed Janak, who first showed interest in my scholarship, regularly made room for me in sessions of the Popular Culture of America's "Education, History, and Popular Culture" interest area, and who secretly gave my wife the call for book proposals, saying, "Make him do this!"

I would also like to thank Ludovic Sourdot, whose collaboration with Dr. Janak helped make this book series possible, and who warmly urged me to stick with the project when some early peer reviews were discouraging.

I would like to thank Judith Lakamper, who answered every single one of my many questions about preparing the manuscript, and Mikayla Mislak who helped shepherd the final draft through to completed publication.

On a more local level, thanks go to Dr. Mariann Tillery, a Dean whose personal friendship, professional trust, and approving signatures made possible much of the foundational work that became this study. Likewise, Dr. Dennis Carroll was my Provost and more importantly my team-teacher during our earliest days of exploring images and ideas of education in popular media. Those ideas could not have been fully developed without weekly conversations with my First Year Seminar students who followed me to Neverland and down the rabbit hole (and back) every semester. It was fun, and these readings are a celebration of our time together in the classroom.

Finally, I must thank Teri Beadle, who loved me through it all and made me write the book.

Introduction

What follows is a book-length study of some of the most popular, familiar, widely loved, and culturally influential works of British children's literature, through the lens of educational theory. It is as if to wonder what these books would say if they were considered as commentaries on education. To experts in either of these areas of scholarship, the readings that follow may seem surprisingly general, perhaps even superficial. However, it is precisely through taking a broader view that I have found the pathways to introduce these two bodies of text to each other and bring them into dialogue, allowing each to inform and enrich the other.

More particularly and personally, these essays grew from two seeds. The first, a series of conversations with my students in a program that was my university's First Year Seminar program. One course I teach in that program, titled, "Images of Teaching in Film, Fiction, and TV," began with my doctoral dissertation, which concluded that teachers are far more consistently influenced by the models and images of teachers available through pop culture, personality, and even whim, than any particular methodology they may have studied in a teacher education program.

The second seed began to germinate through some early runs of another FYS course, this one titled, "The Neverland Variations." That course follows the various literary, cinematic, and theatrical tellings and retellings of *Peter Pan*, *Alice's Adventures in Wonderland*, and *Through the Looking-Glass*. The idea for the course began to germinate on a six-hour road trip with my children to visit their grandparents. To manage the children along the way, I had borrowed a library audiobook of J.M. Barrie's novel, *Peter Pan*. I was sure I knew what I was in for. However, within the first few minutes I became transformed by the richness of detail and background in Barrie's fiction that is completely missing from the two gold standard versions that (at the time)

1

had been passed down through popular culture, Disney's animated film and the live TV broadcast starring Mary Martin.

The combination of being led into popular teacher portrayals and deeper readings into the variations inspired by Barrie's original stories soon caused those two projects to melt together into an expansion from Barrie to other similar British writers, and from the typical array of cinematic teachers I addressed in the "Images . . ." course (Sir, Mr. Chips, Mr. Keating, even Ms. Frizzle) to the teachers I was discovering in my own sort of British invasion. It is by extension of that personal, yet academic tradition that I read the works presented here—as portrayals, within a particular literary tradition, of educational theories and conceptual frameworks.

My hope is to accomplish goals on both sides of that equation. On the one hand, you may be interested in education, but never before have considered these literary works as pertaining to that interest. Please enjoy them as refreshing windows into that topic. On the other hand, you may love the literary works examined here, but never gave much thought to what they say about teaching and learning. This book invites you to return to these classics as an opportunity to think differently, maybe even innovatively, about their respective commentary on education. If you are an expert in a literary area that includes these works, you may not find any great, new contribution to your professional conversation. Likewise, if you are an expert in, say, educational psychology, you may not find any fresh contributions to the research on Piaget or Vygotsky. What you will find, however, are two engaging sources of material brought into dialogue with each other to serve collectively in a humane and aesthetic exercise in a mutually expanding insight. At least, that is my intention. I invite you read with an openness to that outcome.

The chapters address the works in the approximate order they were published, and each opens with a summary of the educational theory that guides the critical reading performed in that chapter. Consequently, the first chapter examines how Lewis Carroll takes his heroine on a journey through cognitive, psycho-social, and moral development. In the second chapter, I consider Beatrix Potter's tales as studies in Progressive Education. Chapter 3 finds the many ways in which *Peter Pan* (both the play and novel) articulates something suggestive of Rousseau's *Emile* and other more contemporary arguments for natural learning. I argue that Barrie, perhaps unintentionally (though often it's hard to think he wasn't intentional), criticizes formal schooling. He cites its peer pressures and competitive systems, intimidating forces linked to professional and social status, as an institution which often leaves lifelong emotional scars, while exploring how more individualized, naturalistic approaches to education honor the imagination and promise lifelong significance. In chapter 4, I explore how Kenneth Grahamme's *The Wind in the Willows* portrays a learning process defined by the continual and recursive experiences of going out, returning home, as well as the aspirational, frightening, and even nostalgic elements of those journeys and cycles. The theoretical framework for that reading will be Plato's Allegory of the Cave, itself an iconic story of an education as painful as it is liberating. Next, I examine Winnie-the-Pooh as A. A. Milne's model for what is now widely referred to as "Growth Mindset," and then C. S. Lewis's *The Lion, the Witch, and the Wardrobe* as a prophetic case study of the abusive effects of high-stakes testing. The final two chapters offer analyses of two sides of the teaching–learning relationship. In chapter 7, "learning" is considered through the theoretical lens of Inquiry (sometimes referred to as "Environmental Inquiry" or "Reflective Practice") through its initially reluctant student protagonist, Bilbo Baggins. Chapter 8 refers to scholarship on teacher identity and personality, through a reading of the dynamic, diverse, and often dramatic faculty of "Hogwarts School for Witchcraft and Wizardry," a reading of the first three novels in Rowling's series.

Ultimately, whether through your background in education this book renews your interest in Barrie or *House at Pooh Corner*, or through your expertise in children's literature you find here a new angle on effective classroom instruction or human development (or, like me, you simply find both of these disciplinary traditions important, interrelated, imminently interesting, at times even beautiful), I hope the journey through these essays animates your imagination, enriches your conversation, and expands your alertness for educational insight.

Chapter 1

Learning Down the Rabbit Hole

Lewis Carroll's Alice Novels as Case Studies of Human Development

INTRODUCTION

As the chapter title indicates, this first educational focus is human development, particularly those theories of development articulated by Lev Vygotsky, Erik Erikson, Lawrence Kohlberg, and Carol Gilligan. Vygotsky studied the processes whereby people develop their cognitive functions using social interaction (specifically language) and mentor support (scaffolding) to narrow the gaps (what he referred to as zones of proximal development) between what they already know and what they need to learn.[1] Erikson, in turn, studied a process whereby people develop in ways he termed, "psychosocial," by resolving (ideally through synthesis and integration) increasingly complex binaries defining one's place in and action upon the world.[2] Providing the third theoretical lens, Lawrence Kohlberg studied the ways in which people's decisions (especially those that affect others) mature as they reflect increasing levels of empathy, integrity, and ethical principles.[3] Following up on Kohlberg's research, Carol Gilligan developed theories of moral development that distinguish value systems by gender, with females favoring conditions such as empathy, fairness, and consensus, while males validate decisions based on the logical application of rules and the determination of a correct answer.[4]

Consequently, in order to learn well, according to this collection of theory, a person must encounter new experiences, be open to perceiving them, notice contrasts with what they have known thus far, and either sort the new experience in or provide new space for it to live, cognitively speaking. Conversation and other kinds of social interaction seem to help, as does the occasional nudging from an expert guide. And, as one learns, the developing self becomes increasingly complex, growing from purely physical and mechanical exercises to cognitive acquisition and understanding and ultimately into abstract realms of identity and morality. In those regards, Alice is no different from any other small human.

THE READING

In the very opening sentence of Lewis Carroll's, *Alice's Adventures in Wonderland*, the book's heroine occupies a beginner's stage of all these developmental dimensions, and that state has already affected her attitude toward learning. Alice is sitting by her sister, who is herself doing homework that lacks any interest for the younger sibling. She becomes bored and lethargic, disappointed in discovering that her sister is studying from a book, "without pictures or conversations?"[5]

Right away, in addition to noticing that what homework needs is something visual (experiential) and something socially (not merely academically) linguistic, Alice seems already to have some understanding of what she would prefer in a book. She has to know at least something about what to look for in order to recognize its absence. Then, the question becomes (as it does with perhaps any revelation of prior knowledge) whether it is the kind of background from which to leap into new learning or from which to retreat into cognitive stasis.

Leaping seems to be the necessary next step, given Alice's state of mind during stasis. She is bored to the point of complete apathy, debating "whether the pleasure of making a daisy-chain would be worth the trouble of getting up and picking the daisies."[6] Even in this "lazy" consideration, Alice is both conscious of her options and is meta-cognitively processing her openness to pursuing those options. Her mind is active, even in (and also, regarding) its initial state of inactivity.

All of that begins to change a moment later when she first sees the White Rabbit. It is an observation that immediately sparks heightened mental activity and "burning with curiosity," a state significantly different from the apathy she was feeling just a paragraph earlier.[7] Fueled by this curiosity, Alice takes action, running across the field to where the Rabbit disappears down its hole. She follows the Rabbit down the hole.

And then, she fell.

She fell and fell, and then she fell some more. Only moments after having an experience that triggered an awakened thought process, and a feeling of burning curiosity, both sensations leading her to action, Alice is in chaos, plummeting without any noticeable sense of control or purpose, just a vivid sense of change. Her situation is not unlike that of a startled infant or a toddler (in Erikson's stage of initiative vs. guilt)[8] or a middle-schooler on his or her first day of Algebra I. Solve for "x." But what, he or she wonders, is "x?"

In this case, Alice does exactly what all of those other students do—she refers to the lessons already learned and currently available to her for figuring things out:

> "I must be getting somewhere near the centre of the earth. Let me see: that would be four thousand miles down, I think—" (for, you see, Alice had learnt several things of this sort in her lessons in the schoolroom, and though this was not a very good opportunity for showing off her knowledge, as there was no one to listen to her, still it was good practice to say it over) ". . . but then I wonder what Latitude or Longitude I've got to?" (Alice had no idea what Latitude was, or Longitude either, but thought they were nice grand words to say.)[9]

This recitation of lessons learned, of prior knowledge, continues through a series of admittedly useless, decontextualized, and usually incorrect examples. The knowledge that she brings to bear on this new experience is merely school-room knowledge, learned apparently not for authentic problem-solving but rather for the purpose of "showing off" to a teacher, presumably in return for praise, a grade, or some other form of approval or flattery. Further, as Vygotsky might observe, Alice has no one to talk with about her knowledge but herself; consequently, she is left to manage on her own with this flawed information, with only the quickly growing sense that it is inadequate to the current task (as interesting and now as inescapable as that task may be).

At the end of the fall, Alice is surprisingly safe. She follows the White Rabbit into a hall of locked doors, doors which only prompt her to wonder how she can possibly get out. This would be her second learning impulse (the first being to follow the White Rabbit in the first place). This moment also is the beginning of a sequence of events which begins Alice's development of intentional, strategic thinking.

First in the sequence is her noticing a glass table on which rests a key. Then, she wonders if the key fits any of the doors, a reasonable connection. Third, she notices (as she had not done originally) an additional door, one which is just the right size for the key, but far too small for her. Problem two: Now that she can open the door, how can she get through it? Or, as Alice thought it to herself, "'I think I could, if I only knew how to begin.' For, you see, so many out-of-the-way things had happened lately, that Alice had begun to think that very few things indeed were really impossible."[10]

It is precisely upon conceptualizing this sense of possibility that Alice sees her next potential solution, a bottle marked with the words, "DRINK ME." She first uses her prior knowledge of bottles, those of which may contain poison (in her awareness) always marked as such, before (upon not seeing any such markings) following the directions on this bottle's label. Again, this step marks the first example of another significant feature of

Alice's growth—the mechanism for controlling herself (in this case, her size). As first steps go, it is carefully guided (or scaffolded). The label provides her with instructions for the bottle's use (later, no such label will be required). The results of this first effort are awkward, to be sure, as Alice immediately shrinks to a height that enables her to pass through the door, but too short, now, to reach the key which is still on the table, visible through the glass above her head.

As if a product of her own awareness, there appears on the floor beneath the table, a cake in a small glass box. The cake is marked, "EAT ME." Already, Alice's thought processes actively at work on the new flow of fresh, stimulating, incoming experience, she reasons, "'if it makes me grow larger, I can reach the key; and if it makes me grow smaller, I can creep under the door; so either way I'll get into the garden, and I don't care which happens!'"[11] It is the last clause of that declaration that indicates her as-yet neophyte status as a learner. She'll be happier simply to get a manageable result than she is interested, for now, in controlling that result to achieve a more specific outcome. That comes later.

Eating the cake, in this case, continues the awkward throes of early learning, as the tiny girl grows to such a height that she begins to cry, and her crying (coming now from such a giant person) creates a "pool of tears" (the title of the novel's second chapter) in which she swims after shrinking again, this shrinking caused by her holding a fan left behind by the White Rabbit. This is yet another relatively random source of control, but as a small sign of progress, it is one that Alice discovers on her own, not one that presents itself with instructions. As she notices herself shrinking, Alice realizes that "the cause of this was the fan she was holding, and she dropped it hastily, just in time to avoid shrinking away altogether."[12] Once she is swimming in her tears, she immediately regrets having cried, suggesting an awareness of the connection between action and consequences that will become increasingly important as Alice learns more about intention and control.

These substantive insights battle predictably with past cases of rote learning (still her more well-established version of education). As she encounters a mouse swimming with her in the pool, she first addresses him in academic terms:

> "she remembered having seen in her brother's Latin Grammar, 'A mouse—of a mouse—to a mouse—a mouse—O mouse!'" Following treating the mouse as a Latin lesson, she turns to history: "'I daresay it's a French mouse, come over with William the Conqueror' . . . so she began again: 'Ou es ma chatte?' which was the first sentence in her French lesson-book."[13] The mouse pushes back with real-life fright over Alice's reference to a cat, for which she apologizes.

The mouse responds, again quite grounded in practical reasoning, "Would you like cats if you were me?"[14]

Neither a mouse nor a cat, in its most relevant form, is a mere topic in a "lesson-book." These are creatures with identity, purpose, and consequence. This is simultaneously one of the many examples (they already are starting to pile up) of Carroll's criticism of formal education and his introduction to a more fully Vygotskyan look at the educational process. With the mouse, Alice has someone with whom to enter into dialogue, bounce ideas off , revise, and expand previously held truth, and navigate an apparently ever-extending series of zones of proximal development. Carroll presents his reader with a protagonist who is beginning (though only still just beginning) to become familiar with the difference between what she knows and what she doesn't and to engage with increasing intention in navigating that zone. Alice's practice of this lesson leads her to greater and greater recognition of the kinds of cakes and drinks that will allow her to control her size. As that process develops, another one is set to begin. It is a process suggested physically by personal size control, and more cognitively by Alice's encounter with an "other," the mouse, who has its own unique traits (it fears cats), as well as in that character's question which culminates with the challenging condition, "If you were me?"

These are all considerations that introduce the importance of the next major domain of learning: Identity. To complete Erikson's theoretical binary, when the Caterpillar first presents her with his famous question, "Who are you?" Alice responds with an expected level of confusion. "I hardly know, sir, just at present."[15] After a series of earlier encounters with characters whose linguistic intention (or at least effect) seems to contradict and obfuscate, Alice finds with the Caterpillar a second conversationalist, one perhaps not entirely as impromptu as the Mouse, but one whose contradictions are rhetorically constructive, and whose challenges are answerable and educational. Put another way, after a sequence of experiences whereby Alice becomes quite adept at adjusting her size to fit current needs, she is beginning a sequence whereby she adjusts her thinking to fit her sense of reason.

The Caterpillar introduces that sequence by presenting her identity as something open to question. The question itself presents the notion that such identity is both debatable and discernable. After an initial attempt to avoid the subject altogether, Alice edges toward an answer by attempting to explain who she is not. For example, she fears that one reason for her uncertainty about her identity is her suspicion that her current height does not fit her reality. The Caterpillar effectively moves her Socratically from a stance of discrediting that height altogether to one which accepts its relative value for someone other than she:

"I can't explain myself, I'm afraid, sir," said Alice, "because I'm not myself, you see."

"I don't see," said the Caterpillar.

"being so many different sizes in a day is very confusing."

"It isn't," said the Caterpillar.[16]

Of course, to the Caterpillar (a creature who spends his entire days stretching and contracting, and who is on his own developmental way toward full blown metamorphosis) the prospect of being different may not be confusing. Unconvinced, Alice explains to the Caterpillar that when he soon forms a chrysalis and then turns into a butterfly, he will feel, "a little queer." The Caterpillar fails to accept her prediction, and so Alice admits, "all I know is, it would feel very queer to *me*"[17]. Ah, progress.

It is a progress clarified through contrast proportionally as her prior school learning is fading. At first, Alice portrays this fade to the Caterpillar as evidence of her uncertainty of her identity, and truly her identity as, "classroom student" may be becoming more and more obviously irrelevant. To prove that she is losing that identity (or more likely to see if it still pertains) she attempts an old school recitation, "You are old, Father William." Her recitation prompts the Caterpillar's critique, but more importantly it prompts him (after proclaiming her recitation, "wrong from beginning to end,") to ask, "What size do you want to be?"[18]. *How often in my own academic career, have I asked a student, "So, do **you** want to go to med school? What do YOU want to major in? What do YOU want to do?"*

The best Alice can muster in the moment is to acknowledge that she would like to be a bit taller, as: "three inches is such a wretched height to be." "'It is a very good height, indeed!' said the Caterpillar angrily," himself being, "exactly three inches high." Proper height, it would seem, is relative to identity. "'But I'm not used to it!' pleaded poor Alice in a piteous tone."[19]

So, she is not *used* to it—an understandable emotional state still so early on this new stage of learning. Then, perhaps foreseeing already Alice's autonomy and intentionality, the Caterpillar leaves her with the following information. "One side will make you grow taller, and the other side will make you grow shorter."[20] In her uncertainty about which side of the mushroom is which (it has, after all, a round cap), Alice forces herself to choose (another leap—or fall—into the unknown), grabbing a clump from each side of the mushroom (she spends the next several episodes of the narrative eating from one hand or the other in order to achieve the very size she wants to be). The balance of the Caterpillar's rhetorical challenges and experiential choices provides Alice with the sort of scaffolding that allows her to hone her practice at making more and more independent choices to create more and more personalized outcomes (at least as far as size and identity are concerned).

With that learning enterprise underway, Alice encounters the next challenging question, one about her next course of direction, which in this case she addresses to the Cheshire Cat. "That depends a good deal," he answers, "on where you want to get to."[21] As Alice quickly learns, if you don't care where you want to arrive then your direction is irrelevant, and if you you're content to arrive simply anywhere then you're sure to succeed. In other words, in this as in most cases of effective education, the going in itself is not the cognitive aim. At least, it's not the aim that matters. Going, the Cat implies, is inevitable. Likewise, arrival naturally follows from going. What matters is the way in which one defines the destination in order to go in the direction that leads to that intention, and consequently to arrive at a spot that fulfills that intention.

As Alice begins to understand who she is and where she wants to go, and as she learns to trust more and more her own capacity to determine what does and doesn't make sense, she is ripe for an encounter with a challenge to that "sense" in the form of those who are declared, "mad." I am referring to the Cheshire Cat's directing her to the Mad Hatter's tea party. The Cat assures her that, "We're all mad here," inviting her to evaluate even her own sanity when, in response to her question, "How do you know I'm mad?" he observes, "You must be . . . or you wouldn't have come here."[22]

No longer the Alice who cries in the face of unexpected outcomes, the Alice of "Chapter Seven" stands toe-to-toe with The Hatter's and March Hare's linguistic reversals and twisted logic, calling out each fallacy, noting each faulty assumption, and arguing as an equal each premise and proposition. If, indeed, "We're all mad here," then madness may well be the knack for sharing divergent views, sorting through their details for strengths and weaknesses, for truth and error, sitting in chaos and engaging in dialogue, not recitation. In that spirit, it's likely that one of Carroll's points (if he does, indeed, have any intentionally educational point) is that only in allowing room for what may be taken for madness can one discover new (what American poet, Emily Dickinson referred to as), "divinest" sense.[23] Put another way, only after one stops merely passing along memorized information, and begins to consider, critique, and really dig into absurd, even-mad-sounding points of view is one beginning to exercise true intelligence and (if it's working properly) a real education.

In that spirit, then, the Cheshire Cat ushers the ever (cognitively) growing Alice to "A Mad Tea Party," (the title of that seventh chapter) hosted by the iconic Mad Hatter. Throughout the party, Alice stands toe-to-toe with the Mad Hatter, Doormouse, and March Hare, in verbal repartee around the likes of riddles, debates of courtesy, logic (and reversals), and complete uncertainty. For even when Alice (thinking there's an answer) realizes that she cannot solve the Hatter's riddle, the Hatter explains, "I haven't the slightest idea," and the March Hare adds, "Nor I."[24] As the scene develops, the verbal nonsense becomes more a case of reasonable (or at least, reasoning), if not completely coherent conversation. The conversation continues this way for another three pages, including Alice's admitting to confusion, though never once backing away from engagement, and culminating in Alice's comment, "I don't think," which is interrupted by the Hatter, "Then you shouldn't talk."[25]

Interestingly, this comment, identified by Alice as "rudeness," ends the conversation, as well as her time at the party. As she leaves, vowing never to return, she proclaims the Mad Hatter's event, "the stupidest tea-party I ever was at in all my life."[26] However, though she seems to have considered the entire experience something of a waste of time, Alice's leaving the party takes her directly back to the hallway where she began, now possessing all the knowledge she needs to move successfully through the small door she failed to enter earlier. It is through this door, appropriately enough, where she finds the Queen's croquet ground, and is brought to trial for stealing the Queen's tarts. Having learned to hold her own in debates of reason and manners, she now will prove her skills at debating such abstractions as justice and being, themselves.

While there is a variety of characters and plot details that stand between her arrival for croquet and the trial, I will jump straight to the trial, as that is the final demonstration of educational achievement portrayed in this first of Carroll's two Alice novels. To review, the sequence began with the move from apathy and sleepiness, with only a slight recognition of what might be better. Then, it was activated by curiosity, albeit a rather unreflective brand of curiosity, which led to something of a freefall, followed by a series of increasingly supported and autonomous efforts at self-control and self-understanding. That state led to the beginnings of Alice's ability to interact with strength and evaluate both her own ideas and those of others. Finally, with the power to manage new situations with strength and clarity, Alice quite literally opens the door to the larger world of experience. It is an experience in which she will find herself on trial, accused of absurd violations by absurd characters, characters whose only authority is external (though they hold titles of queen, king, duchess; not teacher, principal, or superintendent), and whose orders are carried out mindlessly, if at all (does anyone believe that a guard is really going to cut off Alice's head?). It is Alice's final confrontation with traditional authority figures who would pretend to have any claim on her own mind and will. Consequently, at the moment that she recognizes and calls them out as, "nothing but a pack of cards,"[27] the sheer truth of that matter renders them so. By this point in the trial, Alice has even physically grown to full height (a point which is lost, by the way, in the Disney version, which has her shrink again, no sooner than she has reached the height of her powers—perhaps a relic of a more sexist interpretation of little girls' power, and more suitable for another study). Carroll's Alice uses the final moments of the trial to confront her accuser, grow "to her full size," and return surrounded by the flurry of now powerless playing cards to where she began her journey, "lying on the bank, with her head in the lap of her sister."[28]

If that was where she'd stayed, still wondering about the trouble and tedium of making a daisy chain, the story might have turned in on itself. Instead, Alice relives her experience, as if in one sense, to test it, to study it, to make sure it was real and that she still remembers it, but also as way of sharing her story with her sister-now-student. Then, as if having learned from *her* younger sister-now-teacher, Alice's older sibling begins to think about Wonderland, first as she has heard of it from Alice, and then (is it a kernel of her own prior knowledge?), "she sat on, with closed eyes, and half believed herself in Wonderland."[29] To complete the validation of Alice's achievements, Carroll has the sister imagining Alice as an adult, sharing stories of her lessons from Wonderland with the children she would know in those later days, and presumably who would use those stories for their own enchantment and education.

So, Alice has completed her journey through Wonderland. This is the story of the first novel, a story of personal growth in both cognition and identity.

In the second novel, *Through the Looking Glass*, Alice's lessons are launched more intentionally by the prior knowledge and strategic will acquired in the first, and they begin with an invitation to a would-be student (even though it is just her cat): "If you'll only attend, Kitty, and not talk so much, I'll tell you all my ideas about Looking-glass House."[30] Unlike her tumble into the rabbit hole, here Alice already has "ideas," posing questions that indicate not only curiosity but the background for having built that curiosity: "How would you like to live in Looking-glass house, Kitty? . . . Let's pretend there's a way of getting through into it, somehow . . . . Let's pretend the glass has got all soft like gauze, so that we can get through. Why it's turning into a sort of mist now, I declare! It'll be easy enough to get through."[31]

This is the kind of advanced starting point that a reader might expect, having followed Alice through the education she receives in the first novel. She begins *Through the Looking Glass* from the vantage point of that earlier education. Consequently, instead of beginning with the discovery of such simple dimensions as size control or individual identity, Alice enters (once inside Looking-glass House) a world of populations and classifications.

This world introduces itself in the form of chess pieces (counterparts of the cards of Wonderland). Carroll suggests that chess is a far more complex environment than cards, a game played on a field of checks, with a variety of players, each playing a unique role in combination with the others to advance the game. With chess as the model, this book then introduces Alice to the notion of perspective, as the poem "Jabberwocky" appears in a book, but only mirror imaged, so that it needs to be reflected in order to be read.

As in chess, the point of view is essential to decoding the poem, as it is to understanding the whole notion of otherness. This insight prepares Alice for the Garden of Flowers, where she encounters not just one creature (White Rabbit, Caterpillar, or Cheshire Cat) or even a group of distinctive individuals (Hatter, Hare, Door Mouse), but rather whole populations (be they flowers or insects) of the same species of creature, with each presenting its own challenge to perspective, with horseflies (for example) appearing as actual rocking horses, flitting around with literally rendered dragonflies and butterflies. Never mind, "Who are you?" We are now fully immersed in, "Who are they, and they, and *they*?" And by extension, who are we?

As the focus on the individual turns to focus on the population, matters of cognition and identity turn into matters of ethics and justice. For example, the Walrus and the Carpenter invite a group of oysters, first to join them on a walk along the beach, then to dinner, and finally to *become* dinner. Throughout the "walk" the oysters, as a group, are continually reclassified in importance until it becomes clear that their status was never that of equal. As they prepare to eat the oysters, the Walrus comments, "It seems a shame . . . to play them such a trick," and yet, "The Carpenter said nothing but, 'eh butter's spread too thick!'"[32] Both have intended all along on eating the oysters, but only the Walrus acknowledges the injustice, or at least the "shame" in that point. Alice announces, "I like the Walrus best . . . because he was a *little* sorry for the poor oysters." "He ate more than the Carpenter, though," answers Tweedledee.[33] Thus laying out the details for the ethical debate between the one who ate more (and lied about it, to boot) but felt worse, and the one who actually ate less, but was unaffected by the trick, though it affected fewer victims, Carroll writes Alice into one of the novel's noticeable ethical debates, one which instead of resolving as her nonsensical, male counterparts attempt, she examines for its more "human" elements of empathy and authenticity.

In another case, the Mad Hatter in this novel has become a character referred to as, "Hatta," a King's Messenger, reported in chapter 5 ("Wool and Water") of the book as having been imprisoned, "though the trial doesn't even begin till next Wednesday: and of course the crime comes last of all."[34] He reappears in chapter 7 ("The Lion and the Unicorn") with the other King's Messenger, "Haigha" (which, if pronounced with an English accent sounds like, "Hare"). In other words, they have become not just literally present, concrete, as in the first novel, but referential, suggestive of their abstraction. By this point in the narrative, both characters are more explicitly serving (and victims of) the larger narrative context, set as they are in a system of royalty, both as messengers, one as absurdly imprisoned and then released by that royalty and the other who recognizes the absurdity of the system which has imprisoned his friend, yet attempts to translate it.

The Queen who attempts to account for this feature of Looking Glass House explains it as "living backwards," and Humpty Dumpty (found in the chapter entitled with that name) portrays the feature quite rationally in a lengthy examination of the phenomenon of the "un-birthday." It is also in this chapter in which Humpty Dumpty offers a quite detailed but also quite absurd interpretation of Carroll's poem, "Jabberwocky," itself a poem characterized by both absurd language and narrative continuity.

In all these features, Carroll is expanding his wordplay into logical gaming, transforming turns of phrase into systems of reason. It is as if we are in a higher grade in school, increasingly confused, and yet increasingly convinced it is we who are at fault, we who have made the error of understanding. Yet, through this passage, Alice remains alert, engaged, cognizant, open, honest, patient, and interactive. She manages conversation with Humpty, with the Queen, with the Lion, the Unicorn, the Knight, and all other characters who seem to operate through, and consequently to extend, systems of flawed thinking. As a result, and in contrast to the first novel which ends with Alice's being irrationally convicted of being a thief, nearing the end of the second novel, Alice is told she is to be made Queen. The news leaves her quite excited and hopeful, especially as she reaches up to discover that she already is wearing a crown. Her excitement lasts until she runs into the two literal Queens from the chess game. It is this encounter which sets up the finale to the second novel.

The two board queens grill Alice on pedantic, academic details. "Can you do Addition? . . . Can you do Subtraction? Can you do Division?" Alice responds, first with the honest, human need for time to adequately think through the specific problems that the queens toss her way, then with angry, self-righteous retorts, "'Can *you* do sums?' Alice said, turning suddenly on the White Queen, for she didn't like being found fault with so much."[35]

In a separate strand of inquiry, when the Queens ask about bread-making, Alice replies with a reference to flour, at which point the Queens ask about picking the flour (meaning a reference to, "flower") to which Alice replies, "it isn't picked at all . . . it's ground," to which the Queens continue, "how many acres of ground?"[36] So, on goes what in traditional school culture would be considered as the most abusive form of "gotcha" style, "recitation" pedagogy. Yet, as if exiting an array of verbal rapids, the waters gradually calm into a balanced conversation among the three characters, ending in the Red Queen's taking Alice by the hand and saying about her White counterpart, "Your Majesty must excuse her . . . she means well, but she can't help saying foolish things, as a general rule,"[37] a pattern of the Red Queen's behavior that is recognized by the White Queen, and conveyed to Alice as context for understanding the human side of what otherwise appears as verbal abuse.

So with both Queens now solidly in support, Alice is guided to a banquet hall full of guests who all turn out to be chess pieces. In a gesture of acceptance, they ask Alice to "return thanks," before the dinner begins. However, as a way of ushering Alice out of the novel (as she exited the first one) with a final evaluation, the characters all rise to a chaotic din, prompting the heroine to pull away the table cloth, sending the pieces flying and crashing as the inanimate objects that they were. In a final sequence of action, Alice lifts the Red Queen, who transforms into "Kitty" as Alice is returning from Looking-glass House.

A noteworthy difference upon this return is Alice's awareness: "You woke me out of oh! such a nice dream! And you've been along with me, Kitty—all through the Looking-Glass world. Did you know it, dear?"[38] Alice now owns her dream, and isn't just the recipient of it. She acknowledges her own process in navigating the imaginary world, as well as Kitty's likely difference in awareness of that journey. It is a metacognitive as well as ethical state in which Alice understands both her own learning as well as that of one whose experience is different from hers. Aware even of the mechanism of her learning, Alice speaks of reciting the poetry from her dream in order to take Kitty back there through "make believe,"[39] again a small but significant difference from how she left her sister in the first novel to imagine Wonderland from the then younger girl's more innocent recounting of it as reality.

Whether he meant to or not, or whether I am just imagining things myself, or not, as I read Lewis Carroll's two Alice novels, I see the portrayal of a child who moves from sleepy half-awareness and useless, disjointed knowledge to a person who is aware of herself, intentional and strategic in her management of her life, interactive and intelligent in her approach to complexity and confusion, discerning in her identification and treatment of others, and finally, aware of how all of it worked and may continue to work as rules and circumstances change. She has been truly educated, and her education shows signs of some of the most familiar educational theories from the past hundred years—theories of cognitive, psycho-social, and moral development, all brought to bear in a whimsical story about a little girl who happened to wake up, fall down a hole, and discover that, "we're all mad here!"

NOTES

1. Lev Vygotsky, *Thought and Language: Revised and Expanded Edition* (Cambridge: MIT Press, 2012).

2. Erik Erikson, *Childhood and Society* (New York: W. W. Norton and Company, 1950).

3. Lawrence Kohlberg, *The Philosophy of Moral Development* (New York: Harper and Row, 1981).

4. Carol Gilligan, *In a Different Voice: Psychological Theory and Women's Development* (Cambridge, MA: Harvard University Press, 1982).

5. Lewis Carroll, *Alice's Adventures in Wonderland* (London: Puffin Books, 1994), 1.

6. Ibid., 2.

7. Ibid.

8. Erik Erikson, *Childhood and Society* (New York: W. W. Norton and Company, 1950).

9. Lewis Carroll, *Alice's Adventures in Wonderland* (London: Puffin Books, 1994), 3–4.

10. Ibid., 10–11.

11. Ibid., 9.

12. Ibid., 16.

13. Ibid., 18.

14. Ibid.

15. Ibid., 43.

16. Ibid., 44.

17. Ibid.

18. Ibid., 49.

19. Ibid., 49–50.

20. Ibid., 50.

21. Ibid., 64.

22. Ibid., 65.

23. Emily Dickinson, *The Complete Poems of Emily Dickinson* (Boston: Little, Brown and Co., 1960), 209.

24. Lewis Carroll, *Alice's Adventures in Wonderland* (London: Puffin Books, 1994), 73.

25. Ibid., 79.

26. Ibid., 80.

27. Ibid., 135.

28. Ibid., 136.

29. Ibid., 137.

30. Lewis Carroll, *Alice's Adventures in Wonderland and Through the Looking-Glass* (New York: Oxford University Press, 2009), 127.

31. Ibid.

32. Ibid., 165.

33. Ibid., 166.

34. Ibid., 175.

35. Ibid., 226–227.

36. Ibid., 227.

37. Ibid., 229.

38. Ibid., 242.

39. Ibid., 243.

.

Chapter 2

Beatrix Potter as a Champion of Progressive Education

INTRODUCTION

What follows is a close look at the portrayals of three distinctly different models of education. There is what Goodlad calls "frontal" teaching, a student-teacher relationship characterized by lecture and testing. His study identifies this teach-by-telling format as a staple especially of high school pedagogy.[1] Because it is (hallowed or hated) such a long-standing classroom tradition, and because it creates both a formalized and formulaic relationship between teacher and students, I refer to it in this chapter as formal education. It appears in Potter's tales anytime a character pedantically provides verbal directions that are intended and expected simply to be obeyed.

Then, there is what the likes of Dewey,[2] Montessori,[3] and Rousseau[4] each explore as education through and for experience. Here, I call that alternately natural and experiential education. Its students learn from life, and live their lives as a practice and extension of who they are, and what they know and do.

Finally, some students (particularly in the British tradition that is the focus here) pursue education simply as an entitlement of social status, a late adolescent rite of passage for the aristocracy.[5] This was especially true in the England familiar to Beatrix Potter. At best, this educational tradition provides the wealthy few with elite educational access, and consequently, social inclusion, pathways to business and political leadership, membership into prestigious clubs, and influential conversations. At worst, it encourages students to take their education for granted and revel in the privilege it represents.[6] Because its pursuit is a feature of historical identity and social class, I call this phenomenon inherited or birthright education. In Potter's fiction, the characters who occupy the social class most likely to have inherited their education in this manner are portrayed (though sometimes intellectual, and nearly always charming) as inept aristocrats.

Beatrix Potter's tales by turn portray these three kinds of education. Formal education is usually delivered by animal parents. Experiential or natural education is most often pursued by child animals, and often the most mischievous ones, and also by animal "tradesmen" (carpenters, launderers, seamstresses, and farmers). Inherited or birthright education more often than not is connected to age or species, most clearly portrayed by Mr. McGregor (one of the tales' rare humans), but also reflected in such animal characters as Mr. Jeremy Fisher and his friends, Alderman Ptolemy and Sir Isaac Newton; the spoiled and presumptuous Mr. Samuel Whiskers; and Mrs. Tiggy-winkle's unwanted guest, Mr. Jackson.

What I set out to accomplish in this chapter is an examination of how these different educational approaches are portrayed and contrasted, what kinds of outcomes they promise and deliver, and consequently, which approach may be most effective. As is probably evident in the chapter's title, the educational approach that Potter portrays as most suitable for its students, the one that delivers the most substantive results and daily, personal satisfaction, is one that I call natural or experiential, and that John Dewey developed as Progressive Education. It is an approach which emphasizes learning from experience, not pedantry, and learning to accomplish authentic outcomes, not entitled privileges.

As Dewey, himself, put it, "education is not an affair of 'telling' and being told, but an active and constructive process."[7] Or in another statement, "Education is not infrequently defined as consisting in the acquisition of those habits that effect an adjustment of an individual and his environment . . . . But it is essential that adjustment be understood in its active sense of *control* of means for achieving ends."[8] A conference speaker I heard decades ago offered a profound oversimplification of Dewey's philosophy, and yet it speaks both to the core of Dewey's main concept and (because of its essential quality) to its universal and memorable appeal.

"As Dewey might say," the speaker began, "we learn what we do."

If that tenet is so, then those who *do* (one could hypothesize) may be expected to function more knowledgeably, and even more successfully, than those who hesitate or back away from action, those who simply have passed school tests on, say, "things that might be done," and even more successfully still than those whose knowledge is merely a reflection of their birthright and the pathway it cleared for them to attend a certain school, though not at all necessarily promising them any real engagement with life. The following is an exploration of that hypothesis.

THE READING

Flopsy, Mopsy, Cottontail, and Peter go out for the day, all with the same set of instructions from their mother: "You may go into the fields or down the lane, but don't go into Mr. McGregor's garden." She includes a word about consequences that might be interpreted as a word of caution, and as such, a bit of instruction: "Your father had an accident there; he was put in a pie by Mrs. McGregor." As a final instructional send-off, Mrs. Rabbit adds, "Now run along, and don't get into mischief. I am going out."[9] Mrs. Rabbit's approach seems less, "We learn what we do," than, "We learn what we're told," and Dewey already has directly warned us about that.

Nevertheless, we have specific directions, a description of potential consequences for not following the directions, a general reminder about avoiding "mischief," and finally the clear statement that her instruction has concluded and that the expectations are that those directions will be followed without her further involvement. Applying these lessons, we soon learn, depends directly on whether the students are (as are Flopsy, Mopsy, and Cottontail) "good little bunnies," or (as apparently is Peter) "very naughty."[10] If this approach to education is to work, its students must first hear the instruction, accept the promised or implied consequence of disobeying it, and then have the character to apply it without further intervention from the teacher.

I once nearly failed in biology in college. The professor entered the classroom each Monday, Wednesday, and Friday morning, beginning his lecture as he shut the door, lecturing the entire period, and then providing concluding comments only as he left. The syllabus included a section labelled, "Supplemental Readings," along with a series of dates for quizzes to be taken in class. I was blasting my way through a series of Ds and Fs on the quizzes when finally, I asked a classmate of mine who was receiving As just how he did it.

"Study group," he replied. "That's where we really dig down into the textbook chapter and the supplemental readings."

"You actually read the chapter?" I asked.

"It's assigned," he said, squinting as if he couldn't see me clearly much less understand what I was saying. "I don't suppose you read the supplemental readings, either?"

"They're supplemental," I shrugged. "It says so in the syllabus." In high school, all I ever had to do to make an A was study my lecture notes. My college classmate (now, I might add, a successful surgeon) shook his head.

"It *says*, 'Supplemental,' but he includes questions about them on the test. He expects us to listen to him, read the book and the supplemental readings, and then talk about all of that with each other to learn what we need to learn."

He knew this to be true. All the "good little bunnies" knew it to be true, and many of those bunnies were in his study group.

Did I join the study group? Nope, I did the equivalent of what Peter did—in my case, that meant cutting class a lot to drive up to the mountains for hikes, especially on pretty fall Friday mornings. In Peter's case, it meant scampering off straight to Mr. McGregor's garden. While I was in the mountains, I often saw specimens in the woods or creeks of the kinds of plant and animal life we were studying in class. For class, we had to dissect a frog. On one of my mountain treks, I picked up a live frog and let it sit for nearly a minute in the palm of my hand. The dissection was what showed up on the test, not the memory of how cool the frog's skin felt, how rhythmically his throat inflated and retracted, or what his foot pads felt like as he pushed off and leaped away.

How does that translate to Peter? While he doesn't ignore directions and head off to the mountains, he does something even bolder. It is as if Dr. Allen (or my classmate, his proxy) had warned, "Whatever you do, just don't cut class and go hiking." However, that sort of defiance is precisely what Peter chooses. Since he is, as I have already mentioned, "very naughty," instead of behaving himself, Peter goes straight to Mr. McGregor's garden, and "squeezed under the gate!"[11] That he has to squeeze implies that his efforts were quite intentional and done with some determination. Once he is there, he does what all rabbits do: he eats. In fact, Peter seems to know his way quite well around a vegetable garden, regarding food as well as medicinal herbs, the latter of which he samples after his overindulgence appears to have left him with a tummy ache. In other words, his exploration of Mr. McGregor's garden isn't just some random, disobedient lark. It is a purposeful pursuit guided by a combination of his natural interests and appetites, and his background knowledge of what may be found in vegetable gardens.

Peter's trip into the garden, however, is only the first part of the story, and only the first illustration of his education. A more challenging lesson is presented by Mr. McGregor's discovery of the little rabbit, and of the gardener's giving chase to capture the pest. In short, Peter then must not only know where to find food, what to eat, and how to remedy a belly-ache, but then how to escape once he is caught. Here again, he applies a combination of natural and learned attributes. Rabbits are fast, and they know better than a grown human how to run and hide. Additionally, Peter also knows how to look for options, ask for help, and improvise when things go wrong.

Immediately upon being discovered, Peter runs around in a panic, trying to find his way back to the gate. However, even this detail implies that he is aware that there is a gate and a way back to it. Then, he loses his shoes and gets his jacket button tangled up in a gooseberry net. As a way to regain his freedom to escape, Peter sheds the coat. Given that Peter already has lost his shoes, it doesn't require much of a leap to notice Potter's contrast between the artifice of Peter's human clothing (provided him by his mother, whom we already have noted represents formal education) and his natural rabbit state, far more mobile and better able to solve the problem that his educational environment has presented.

In this natural state, Peter is better able to maneuver and hide until he locates Mr. McGregor, and then wait for just the right moment to run home. And his mother praises his efforts at discovery, grit, and resourcefulness, right? Not at all. Mrs. Rabbit's exasperation at her son's missing clothing is implied in the narrator's voice, "It was the second little jacket and pair of shoes that Peter had lost in a fortnight!"[12] What that statement also implies is that just two weeks earlier, Peter had enjoyed a similar adventure. It would seem that Peter has a penchant for shedding his formal wear in pursuit of his nature, a penchant which creates ongoing inconvenience for his mother, whose ideas about Peter's education are quite different from the ones he pursues. After all, not all learning pleases the teacher.

For all the lessons I may have received about nature on my hiking trips, I still got a D in biology.

"The Tale of Benjamin Bunny" operates as a sequel to "The Tale of Peter Rabbit," and yet its messages about education develop quite differently, and I will argue that they privilege Mrs. Rabbit, and Benjamin's father, "Old Mr. Bunny." The plot of Benjamin Bunny's tale begins with Benjamin noticing the McGregors going out for the morning. He goes to his aunt's house, avoiding her but finding his cousin, Peter. Peter, still sitting wrapped in a pocket handkerchief, explains to Benjamin how he lost his clothes at the McGregor's, and Benjamin, explaining McGregors' outing, suggests that the two bunnies go over to recover Peter's clothes. They can see from the garden wall that the lost garments, along with Mr. McGregor's tam o' shanter, have been used to dress a scarecrow. Peter recovers his lost clothing, then the two bunnies gather onions into the handkerchief and begin to wander around. Eventually, they come upon the McGregors' cat and hide from him under a basket. The cat has no sooner trapped the bunnies under the basket than Old Mr. Bunny arrives. Mr. Bunny fights the cat and locks him in the garden shed, then whips the two bunnies before escorting them home, leaving the returning Mr. McGregor baffled at how his cat could become locked up in the shed, with the door latched from the outside.

That's the plot. However, in the story's details the power and nature of knowledge is portrayed not through, in this case, the young bunnies, but rather in the rabbit adults—adults who, again in this case, don't just offer advice but rather act on experience and nature. This new emphasis begins with what we learn early on about Mrs. Rabbit, not (as before) that she is some sort of absentee rule announcer, but rather that, "she earned a living knitting rabbit-wool mittens and muffetees."[13] The narrator even acknowledges having, "once bought a pair at a bazaar."[14] The reader also learns that Mrs. Rabbit, collects, dries, and sells herbs. This is Mrs. Rabbit's only appearance in Benjamin Bunny's tale, but it does redefine her household presence, while offering a contrasting foil for the two young rabbits, as Benjamin intentionally avoids his aunt and Peter decides to go for a walk, presumably to get out of the house so bustling with practical activity. So because the boys' behavior stands in contrast with the substantive life portrayed around the Rabbit home, their adventure becomes an example of what a teacher might call straying, "off task." Even their garden exploration involves not the kind of intentional tasting and medicating that Peter enjoyed earlier, but a careless gathering of onions (which they continue to drop from their makeshift sack). Old Mr. Bunny's arrival reinforces this contrast.

By that time, unlike Peter's earlier curious, solo exploration of the garden, the two young rabbits have gotten themselves into a fix. They have been caught by the cat and are trapped by him under a basket. The situation calls for outside help, and from someone with the ability to fight effectively with a grown cat. Enter Mr. Bunny, fully equipped with a switch and a rabbit's own natural weapons, claws and two strong back legs. "He took a tremendous jump off the top of the wall on to the top of the cat, and cuffed it off the basket, and kicked it into the green-house, scratching off a handful of fur."[15]

I could at this point offer the conclusion that, once again, natural and pragmatically applied learning won the day. Three particular details from the narrative, however, bear closer examination. First of all, after vanquishing the cat to the shed, Mr. Bunny locked him inside. How did he manage that, given a rabbit's distinct lack of opposable thumbs, much less the height needed for reaching a shed latch? Second, even as he arrives, Mr. Bunny is smoking a pipe and wearing clogs, not exactly the natural (dare I say, au naturel?) state that his young nephew achieved in the earlier tale. Third, once the young rabbits are safe, they are also punished with lashes from Mr. Bunny's switch, much more as would befit a traditional schoolmaster than a Progressive educator. What's going on here?

First of all, the children in the second tale weren't actively learning against a backdrop of superficial instructions, they were playing around against a backdrop of meaningful activity. Arguably, even Mr. Bunny's' switch wielding is just such a meaningful activity (as much as it is a hint of pedagogical traditionalism) because it is applied directly in response to their very unmindfully putting themselves into life-threatening trouble. I mean, cats do eat rabbits, especially when the cat is big and the rabbits are young. As for the pipe and clothing, I see only a blurred line that Potter often treads between natural realism and the fact that her stories are intended for human beings (one human being in particular, her niece). Considering the tales metacognitively for a moment, it could be that dressing up her rabbits in people's clothing, especially in the specific context of this tale, is Potter's comment on the unavoidable artifice in any educational agenda. As if to say, education is contrived, but why not contrive it as realistically as possible? Neither Mrs. Rabbit nor Mr. Bunny is dressed for a fancy ball, after all; they are dressed in the clothes of their working day. By contrast again with the earlier tale, it seems that Peter's earlier clothing is more decorative than functional, which is why Potter narrates him out of it when he needs to accomplish a real task.

Speaking of clothing, human beings, and working woodland creatures, consider now "The Tale of Mrs. Tiggy-winkle," a soft-spoken hedgehog who serves the community as a laundress. We meet Mrs. Tiggy-winkle through the errant wanderings this time of a little human, Lucie. As the tale opens, Lucy has gone out, first into the farmyard and then into the countryside, looking for her most recently misplaced handkerchief. She follows a trail of animals each of whom she asks (to no avail) about having seen the handkerchief. Eventually, she comes to a spring where water is running into a tin can. We soon learn that the can is collecting water for a washerwoman, whom Lucie hears singing to herself as she works. The singing comes from a door "straight into the hill." Knocking on the door, Lucie discovers "a nice clean kitchen with a flagged floor and wooden beams—just like any other farm kitchen. Only the ceiling was so low that Lucie's head nearly touched it; and the pots and pans were small, and so was everything there."[16] Continuing the mystery, the woman who had been singing, and who now pleasantly greets Lucie, is described as having a "little black nose," twinkling eyes, and "underneath her cap—where Lucie had yellow curls—that little person had PRICKLES!"[17]

By way of introduction, Mrs. Tiggy-Winkle describes herself as, "an excellent clear-starcher,"[18] continuing on with her work while she and Lucie chat. Their conversation focuses mainly on the variety of laundry projects that the hedgehog is attending to, each one connected not only with a specific client from the woods, but also with a specific purpose for the garment, and the reason for its needing her care.

As might be predicted, Lucie spots her handkerchiefs, as well as her pinafore (misplaced earlier). She also spots the pocket handkerchief that Peter Rabbit used in the earlier tale to carry the onions. As she continues working, Mrs. Tiggy-winkle explains to Lucie each next washing and starching technique, as well as something about each article of clothing, and when she is done, they have tea by the fire. As the tale ends, Mrs. Tiggy-winkle ties up all of the various bundles of laundered clothes, stokes her fire, locks her door, and hides the key, and Lucie follows her as she delivers her finished products. But then, with only her own collection of cleaned handkerchiefs, Lucie watches as Mrs. Tiggy-winkle disappears up the hill. As the washerwoman disappears from sight, Lucie finally sees her as the simple hedgehog that she has been all along. The narrator concludes with a note that most people would think that Lucie had fallen asleep and dreamed the entire experience, but the cleaned and folded pocket handkerchiefs (along with the narrator's own faithful testimony) suggest that Lucie's encounter was quite real. So, what did it teach her?

The first point of educational analysis should be to identify Mrs. Tiggy-winkle as the teacher. Through both example and explanation, she teaches Lucie about how clothes are taken care of (a lesson that the child seems seriously to need) and about how vocation serves a community as well as a practitioner. As with "The Tale of Peter Rabbit," this tale portrays an importance of the natural in any useful human endeavor, thus Mrs. Tiggy-winkle's appearing to Lucie as simply a peculiar person long before she becomes suspicious that the washerwoman is, in fact, a hedgehog. Even in the context of personhood, the identity of Mrs. Tiggy-winkle operates AS IF the woman is also a hedgehog, as she is described both in human clothing and with prickles sticking through from the inside out. Lucie finds it both confusing and acceptable, an apt metaphor perhaps for any new learning experience.

That Lucie sees the teacher in the end for the pure animal that she is, while the girl now returns to her home human having found what she went into the countryside looking for (her lost handkerchiefs), suggests that Lucie has learned the lesson. The moment has passed successfully, no assessments needed—just the narrator's reminder that the experience was real.

A very different sort of well-dressed animal is Mr. Jeremy Fisher. He and his friends Sir Isaac Newton (a newt) and Alderman Ptolemy Tortoise represent the third sort of education I mentioned at the outset, birthright education. Different from either Mrs. Rabbit's formal directions or Mrs. Tiggy-winkle's model of experience, the inherited education is more a matter of social rank and professional title than of useful knowledge or skill.

"The Tale of Mr. Jeremy Fisher" begins with the gentleman frog noticing how pleasantly wet and slippery the day is, and deciding to go fishing for some minnows to serve to his dinner guests, pretentiously named Sir Isaac and Alderman Ptolemy. The imagery begins with a similarly blurred human/animal boundary, with Mr. Jeremy dressed in snappy clothes, and preparing to punt out into the lake, but his boat naturally being a lily pad, and his pole a section of reed. Likewise, he wants to serve his guests a fine mess of minnows, yet he also acknowledges that Alderman Ptolemy, a tortoise, will only eat salad, as tortoises are herbivores. It's when he is out on the water that Mr. Jeremy's practical knowledge of how to accomplish his goals are proven to be sorely lacking, and interfered with besides by his greater attention to the condition of his galoshes, Macintosh, and lunch basket than to the knowledge of nature and angling needed to catch a minnow.

For, while he is fishing for minnows, a minnow is the one thing he doesn't catch. First, he "landed little Jack Sharp, the stickle-back, covered with spines."[19] Then, he reels in "a great big enormous trout," that "seized Mr. Jeremy with a snap . . . and then it turned and dived down to the bottom of the pond."[20] In fact, the only thing that saved Mr. Jeremy from becoming the trout's lunch was that it didn't like the taste of him and so spat him out. So much for the fishing trip, which seems to be an inconsequential outcome, as Mr. Jeremy feeds his guests adequately (while the Alderman brought his own salad) on "roasted grasshopper with lady-bird sauce; which frogs consider a beautiful treat."[21]

Between the botched fishing skills and the ultimate lack of usefulness of even having fish for dinner at all, the tale presents a character relatively devoid of substantive intention, and consequently relatively uninterested in substantive outcomes of his intended task. It was rather a lark, as are many of the educational enterprises of those whose education is an entitlement merely for providing or identifying status or station.

Potter portrays a similarly presumptuous character (also an older gentleman, and also in this case, an animal), in the "The Tale of Samuel Whiskers, or The Roly-Poly Pudding." It is in this tale that she includes a character who ranks among her very finest examples of Progressive-ism. But he appears much later in the tale. First, consider the protagonist, Tom Kitten, and his mother, Mrs. Tabitha Twitchit.

This tale's beginning is something of a reiteration of the opening of Peter Rabbit, only with less of a didact for a mother than a worrying controller. Rather than give her children instructions, as Peter's mother did, then leave them alone to follow or learn from that instruction, Mrs. Twitchit, "determined to shut them up in a cupboard"[22] while she focused on her day's baking. As un-empowering as it is, physical confinement is more reliable than trusting students to follow directions as a method of behavior management. The only problem is, Tom has already wandered off. Then, like so many teachers with only one trick in their repertoire, all Mrs. Twitchit can do once her confinement plan has failed is to wring her hands and complain to her Cousin Ribby, who reminds her that the Tom is "a bad kitten."[23] Such teachers' lounge talk!

In this model, good instruction controls bad students. When that control breaks down, bad students simply remain "bad." However, this tale ups that ante; the controlling efforts not only fail to teach the desired behavior (in this case, staying out of the way while Mom is baking) but merely prompt the "bad student" to avoid the control. Thus, Tom Kitten doesn't just run away to have an adventure instead of being controlled. That might be (as in Peter's case) a successful lesson in spite of its original plan. Instead of being controlled, Tom might opt to run away to pursue his own experience. By contrast, this bad kitten runs away simply to avoid being confined. In short, he determines not so much to seek adventure, as to hide. This determination led him to discover the space up the chimney above the stove, and it is up that chimney that he discovers Anna Maria and Samuel Whiskers, a rat couple living inside the floorboards of the room above the kitchen.

Samuel, like his narrative counterparts Mr. Jeremy Fisher and friends, is an older character whose education provides privilege (or at least the pretense of it) and not much else. He sees the young Tom and decides that his wife, Anna Maria, must bake the delicacy into a "roly-poly pudding." Anna Maria scurries around gathering all of the necessary ingredients while her husband "takes snuff" and complains that his wife isn't working quickly enough, nor making it "properly."[24] A debate ensues about whether the pudding (in this English context, a meat pie) should have a crust made of dough or bread crumbs, then once they have gathered the proper ingredients for dough and roll Tom into a dumpling, the old rat questions his wife's use of a string to tie the product together (rendering poor Tom looking like a cross between a burrito and an egg roll, with his head coming out one end and his feet the other). The string/no string argument evolves (or devolves) into one about whether the kitten will taste good at all, given that, in Samuel's opinion, "It smells sooty."[25] Just as Anna Maria prepares to counter that point, noise comes from above them, and afore promised, truly Progressive teacher enters the tale.

John Joiner is two times over practical. First of all, he is a terrier, a natural hunter of rats. Second, he is portrayed as a carpenter, precisely the kind of tradesman needed to remove a kitten from between floor joists. Hearing the noise above them, the rats flee. Removing the floorboards, Joiner discovers their abandoned lair confirms through his power of smell their having been there and left, makes the proper repairs, and is rewarded for his services with an invitation to stay for dinner. In other words, he takes care of business.

One might wonder just how it is that John Joiner, while clearly the perfect helper for the problem presented in this tale, is also a teacher. I would argue, to support that claim, that as the one character with a solution (Mrs. Twitchit only wrings her hands, and her cousin does little more than say, "What do you expect from a bad kitten?"), Mr. Joiner brings to the moment examples of skill and problem-solving. Thus, like Mrs. Tiggy-Winkle before him, John Joiner both illustrates the value of his own natural talents and education, as he models their practical applications. What remains is to wonder whether anyone has learned from his lessons. Answering that question will depend on what outcomes one considers valid. If it is ratting and (in this particular case) carpentry, then the theory I am pushing would note that neither good nor bad kittens, nor even the two adult cats, are natural ratters as is Mr. John Joiner, nor are they natural builders as he is portrayed through his "Scottish" terrier persona. However, the point is not that they learn to become him, but that they learn to better live as themselves—solve their own problems, using their own gifts developed in the school of experience. Because of Mrs. Twitchit's open appreciation for Mr. Joiner, as well as her offering him a meal and Tom Kitten a bath, it appears that she is managing her responsibilities differently now than she was at the first of the tale. Originally, she locked her children up simply in order to do some baking. In the end, she not only baked the pudding (from what's left over from the rats' failed effort), but also, "put Tom into a hot bath to get the butter off."[26] I'd say that's progress, perhaps even Progressive.

"The Tale of the Flopsy Bunnies," has one of the simplest plots of all of Potter's tales. Mr. McGregor has been mowing. The Flopsy Bunnies eat some lettuce and then fall asleep in the freshly mown grass. Mr. McGregor finds them and puts them in a bag to take home to Mrs. McGregor. To foil his plan, mice chew a hole in the bag and replace the sleepy bunnies with rotten vegetable rinds. So, when Mrs. McGregor opens the bag in front of her smug, proud husband, she finds the rotten vegetables instead of the tasty bunnies, and gets angry at her husband, while the mice and rabbits all flee to freedom. The end. And yet, the details offer a rich educational landscape.

On the day in question, the Flopsy Bunnies were exploring Mr. McGregor's "rubbish heap," where they found a variety of quite delicious (by bunny standards) clippings left behind by Mr. McGregor's pruning and weeding. After having their fill, "they were overcome with slumber, and lay down in the mown grass."[27] Ever nod off in class? Especially just after lunch? On a warm day, maybe late in the spring, just before school let out for the summer? It's a natural response, just as apparently is sleeping after eating lettuces for a rabbit. An understanding teacher might even schedule in a nap time, or at least some sort of light activity for such an occasion. In this case, however, enter Mr. McGregor, yet another example of privileged, inept education. Instead of nurturing his students, he catches them, his whole plan a power driven, extended "gotcha" moment. He notices the bunnies when, as a fly lands on one of their noses, the nose moves. Finding all of the little Flopsy Bunnies, Mr. McGregor places them giddily into sack as they continue to sleep.

Fortunately for the bunnies, their father, Benjamin Bunny is nearby, as is Mrs. Thomasina Tittlemouse, whom I will discuss in more detail in my next and last reading. When Mrs. Bunny came by on her way home, Mr. Bunny and Mrs. Tittlemouse report that her bunnies are trapped in the bag. Using a resourcefulness that becomes even more apparent shortly, the mouse nibbles through the bag, and the two adult bunnies refill it with "three rotten vegetable marrows, an old blacking-brush and two decayed turnips."[28] This bag of garbage, not a collection of fresh bunnies, is the gift that Mr. McGregor, gloating proudly, presents to his wife. When Mrs. McGregor opens the bag, she thinks her husband has given her the rotten vegetables as a joke, and the two of them are left arguing about it while the bunnies head safely home.

So, once again, the educational establishment is proven completely inept and the power of in-the-moment observation and problem-solving, combined with natural ability (mice excel at chewing through the bags) provide exactly what the situation requires. In her own tale, Mrs. Tittlemouse's resourcefulness is pitted directly against that icon of privilege and presumption, the pompous and oblivious toad, Mr. Jackson.

That tale's plot is possibly even simpler still—Mrs. Tittlemouse is trying to clean her house, and she keeps finding pests, including Mr. Jackson, who simply won't cooperate with her efforts to accomplish her goals. The complexity of the house, itself, with "yards and yards of sandy passages, leading to storerooms and nut-cellars, all amongst the roots of the hedge,"[29] makes the space difficult to manage and the intruders easy to go untended. Beetle, ladybug, spider, bumblebee, all are revealed as the exasperated Mrs. Tittlemouse tries to clean the spaces. Then, Mr. Jackson, having wandered in during her battle with the spiders and bees, already is sitting in the parlour when she finds him.

First, Mrs. Tittlemouse offers her guest a snack of cherry stones, but as toads have no teeth, he cannot eat those. However, still interested in snacking, Mr. Jackson goes off in search of more palatable fare and makes an even greater mess of the house that Mrs. Tittlemouse is trying to clean. After he has decided that bumblebees are too bristly for him to eat, the little mouse scolds the lot of them and shuts herself up in her nut-cellar. When she finally comes out of hiding, she finds a shocking mess: "smears of honey; and moss, and thistle-down—and marks of big and little dirty feet—all over my nice clean house!"[30] This is Mrs. Tittlemouse's moment of taking full and honest stock of her situation. Her previous neglect had allowed too many interlopers, and her politeness had only allowed one of those interlopers to use her house as his own. In teacher terms, she "smiled" before Christmas, tried harder to be liked than to be effective, or perhaps she was, like many either new or burned-out teachers, too interested in addressing the demands of the moment to plan proactively.

However, "Next morning," with apparently fresh resolve, "she got up very early and began a spring cleaning which lasted a fortnight."[31] Or in teacher terms—next Monday morning, she presents her class with a new set of classroom rules and activities that impose order and focus on authentic, useful goals. She cleans out all of the corridors of her home, or, in teacher terms, imagines all of the questions her students may ask and anticipates all of the opportunities they may find to go, "off task." Every action that Mrs. Tittlemouse takes contributes heartily to reclaiming and cleaning her house. This is once again Mrs. Tittlemouse's domain, as any effective classroom teacher's space must be in order for them to establish rapport and facilitate student learning. Grasping this attitude and resolve, she determines effective ways to get things done.

As for Mr. Jackson and his educational tradition, as a student he is still allowed "in class," but not entirely in the house (where he has proven to be so disruptive). Mrs. Tittlemouse has made her door too small for him simply to wander in, but has left it open so that when she has her party to celebrate finishing her cleaning, he has a spot outside by a window, "and he was not at all offended."[32] As a representation of that inherited form of education in general, Mr. Jackson (unlike Mr. Jeremy or Mr. McGregor before him) reflects the openness to methods that draw upon practical goals, pragmatic activity, and human consequence, not just the whimsical pursuit of his own appetites. He is perhaps so inclined to this openness because (again, unlike his predecessors) Mr. Jackson isn't ever simply acting alone (like Mr. Jeremy) or at the expense of others (as with Mr. McGregor or Samuel Whiskers) but in cooperation with Mrs. Tittlemouse. It would seem that her original openness to his intrusion is the seed of his openness to her agenda. As the tale concludes, "He sat outside in the sun, and said—'Tiddly, widdly, widdly! Your very good health, Mrs. Tittlemouse!'"[33]

Or, in student talk, "Thanks for never giving up on me!"

To wrap this up, I want to return to where I started, with a claim that Beatrix Potter supports Progressive Education by contrasting it with a pedantic sort of formal education on one hand and an inherited or privileged form of education on the other. When "students" are given instruction about what to do, they typically ignore it and pursue their own educational adventures. What they learn tends to be guided by who they are, what they can naturally do, and what they find interesting. When they fail to learn, it's often when they pay more attention to reacting against the "instruction" than to the substance of the instruction, or when they fail to take their own interests seriously, or when they are the unassuming victims of the pretentious and entitled forces of privilege.

Within the "faculty" created by Beatrix Potter, some are more effective than others, as some do at least allow their students the opportunities and freedoms either to follow instructions or stray off on their own. Those teachers appear to have some substance to their directions, as (for example) Mrs. Rabbit refers to her deceased husband as evidence of the validity of the warning she offers her children. Others from that "faculty" are, themselves, so unsure of their instruction, so lacking in confidence and authority even in the method they have chosen that rather than leave their students to obey or explore, they prompt them to rebel, thus escaping the teacher's influence by going precisely into the trouble she has tried to warn against.

These "students" are among those who may become the adults of inherited education, lacking in the authentic skills that would allow them to manage their own environment well, and feeling successful simply to have avoided (or made excuses for) a problem (as with Mr. McGregor once he sees he rotten vegetables instead of fresh rabbits, or Mr. Fisher when having botched a fishing trip completely abandons his quest for a fish dinner, or Mr. Samuel Whiskers once discovered mid-dumpling by John Joiner). But even if this model isn't always the necessary extension of reacting against oppressive pedantry, and more of an extension of one's sense of educational entitlement, it shows a kind of learning that prepares one not for the challenges of life, but rather for the trappings of status. It might even be the kind of education that Lucie escapes when she wanders off into the woods to find her pocket handkerchiefs, and in the wandering finds one of the tales' finest models of industry, purpose, and knowledge.

Only the characters like Mrs. Tiggy-winkle who are prepared to manage their daily world and contribute their natural and developed gifts back to their community are portrayed in Potter's tales as being fully engaged, and presumably effectively educated. What she does works, what she does matters. She along with the John Joiner's, Mr. Bunny's, and Mrs. Tittlemouse's of Potter's literary countryside show an awareness of what they are encountering in their moment-by-moment day, and have the intelligence and disposition to be productive and personally fulfilled.

Thus, while there is no direct reference to John Dewey in these tales, I enjoy noting that Dewey and Potter walked the earth at approximately the same time in history, and seem (as I have just attempted to argue) to have developed similar values regarding the processes and benefits (and hazards) of education.

NOTES

1. John I. Goodlad, *A Place Called School: Prospects for the Future* (New York: McGraw-Hill Book Company, 1984).

2. John Dewey, *Democracy and Education* (New York: The Free Press, 1966).

3. Maria Montessori, *The Absorbent Mind* (New York: Holt, Rinehart, and Winston, 1967).

4. Jean-Jacques Rousseau, *Emile, or On Education*, ed. Allan Bloom (New York: Basic Books, 1979).

5. Robert Anderson, "Elite Formation and Excellence in Modern Britain," *Annalie della Scula Normale Superiore de Pisa. Classe di lettere e Filosofia* 3, no.1 (2011).

6. Ibid.

7. John Dewey, *Democracy and Education* (New York: The Free Press, 1966), 38.

8. Ibid., 46.

9. Beatrix Potter, *The Complete Tales of Beatrix Potter* (London: Penguin Random House, Frederick Warne & Company, 1989), 11.

10. Ibid., 12.

11. Ibid.

12. Ibid., 20.

13. Ibid., 56.

14. Ibid.

15. Ibid., 66.

16. Ibid., 90.

17. Ibid.

18. Ibid., 91.

19. Ibid., 126.

20. Ibid., 127.

21. Ibid., 130.

22. Ibid., 175.

23. Ibid., 177.

24. Ibid., 188.

25. Ibid., 187–190.

26. Ibid., 192.

27. Ibid., 200–201.

28. Ibid., 204.

29. Ibid., 225.

30. Ibid., 232.

31. Ibid., 233.

32. Ibid., 234.

33. Ibid.

Chapter 3

The Neverland Academy

Formal Schooling versus Natural Learning in Peter Pan

INTRODUCTION

Finding a modern source in Rousseau's *Emile*[1] and working its way through the twentieth century from Ivan Ilych[2] to near cult status thanks to the works of John Holt[3] and John Taylor Gatto,[4] the idea that children are best educated when becoming most authentically themselves is neither new nor the exclusive domain of advanced academics. It is a driving force behind many student-centered classrooms and project-based curricula, as well as the growing popularity of home schooling and "unschooling."

Ilych focuses primarily on the ways in which oppressive and bureaucratic educational institutions ironically work directly against how people normally learn, proposing instead a combination of teamwork, practical applications, and experience.[5] Holt, perhaps because he was not primarily a scholar but a former classroom teacher, spoke on that same matter in more personal terms. Pondering, "How Children Learn," he concludes that they certainly do not learn via the organized, linear, and segmented programs utilized in school curricula, but rather via a freedom to respond to their own interests, set their own pace, pursue their own need, as presented to them by their own real circumstances.[6] His work has inspired the proliferation of homeschooling and unschooling educational support systems, perhaps the most widely circulated one being the publication and website, *Growing Without Schooling*.[7] Holt's work and proteges provide parents with both the inspiration and the resources to celebrate educating their children as naturally curious individuals (much as was young Emile) unfettered by the artificial constraints of school. Gatto takes this theoretical push against formal education down a path more directly and aggressively critical of the institution of public school, though (like Holt) he is a former classroom teacher. Gatto describes an intentional and

35

nefarious agenda inflicted by formal education on generation after generation of unsuspecting students. This agenda, he argues, is to teach students not academics nor socialization (at least, not in any positive way) but confusion, compliance, dependency, and mediocrity.[8] In Gatto's view, "good" school students (meaning those who are successful within the system, those whom the system likes, and who become what the system is designed to produce) are denied any active participation in what they learn, and are taught to allow the school system to encroach even on their personal, private lives beyond the boundaries of the school day (a.k.a., homework). The more we comply with that model, he argues, the more we lose our true selves.[9]

Whether through direct references to education and school, or portrayals of success and failure, happiness and despair, the education that doesn't work in Barrie's literary world is that which denies, even abuses, the self through school culture and structures, or that which fails to appreciate and nurture all stages of the authentic self, even "growing up" into adulthood. However, neither growing up, nor the story's popularized resistance to it, is exactly where Barrie's narrative actually begins.

THE READING

"I won't go to bed, I won't. I won't."[10] For most people familiar with *Peter Pan*, Michael's defiant proclamation opens the story, there in the nursery on the fateful night when the Darling children fly away to Neverland with their impish leader. They are, in fact, the first spoken lines from the play. However, even in the play version, these lines appear after two pages of exposition and are followed by over half a page of stage direction. In Barrie's novel, the lines that open the play don't appear until two pages into chapter 2. So, whether as a play or a novel, the story doesn't begin, as memory may have it, with the petulant "student" not following restrictive, arbitrary directions, but rather with a first glimpse of the novel's first "teacher," Mrs. Darling, who according to that opening exposition and stage direction, spends most nights "tidying up her children's minds."[11] It is with an examination of that process where I will begin my look at Barrie's portrayals of teachers and schooling.

In the play's notes, this tidying is compared with treating the sleeping children, "as if they were drawers . . . repacking into their proper places the many articles of the mind that have strayed during the day."[12] The overall result is each child's opportunity to "wake in the morning, the naughtiness with which they went to bed . . . placed at the bottom of the drawer; and on the top, beautifully aired, are the prettier thoughts ready for the new day."[13] The novel goes into more detail than simply the analogy to furniture in explaining just where exactly these mindscapes exist.

First, Barrie adds that mind-tidying is being done by mothers each night, all over the world, each mother with each of her respective children. This detail sets him up to speculate just what it is that each mother finds in the process—how each child's mind is different from the other, each day's clutter different, and each tidied result a bit different. In that context, he considers what it must be like to draw a map of a child's mind, imagining the variations differing one from the other. He compares the differences between one mind and another to, "roads on the island, for the Neverland is always more or less an island."[14] Just like that, Barrie introduces the connection between the child's mind and the territory of Neverland, a territory that is fully and uniquely accessible to mothers whose only goal is the tidying up of minds.

If that model, one in which each Neverland may be found in the mind by the tidying mother/teacher, suggests that each child's Neverland is uniquely his or her own, the narrator reinforces that reading in the very next paragraph, pointing out differences across John's, Michael's, and Wendy's Neverlands, offering the kinds of details that reflect, in fact, each child's personality and interests. It was on just such a night, on just such a journey through those Neverlands, when Mrs. Darling discovered, "the word *Peter*."[15]

To review: Mrs. Darling is in the regular habit of tidying up her children's minds as they go to sleep. That sleep is the domain where Neverland exists, each Neverland belonging to each individual child, and no detail there ever being added (by mandate or curriculum) or removed as deficiency, just rearranged so that the good parts (each particular child's good parts) are on top, "beautifully aired." It is in this sort of visit to Neverland where Mrs. Darling first discovers a bit of mind clutter (so to speak) as she tidies, and that clutter is a reference to Peter Pan. This lineage seems important, and it may be explained by starting a few paragraphs earlier in the novel, as we are first introduced to Mrs. Darling as, "a lovely lady, with a romantic mind and such a sweet mocking mouth," with, "one kiss on it that Wendy could never get, though there it was, perfectly conspicuous in the right hand corner."[16] With all the references soon to come of Wendy's offering Peter a kiss, and his giving her one in return (the acorn that soon would save her from Tootles' arrow), it seems reasonable to wonder if Mrs. Darling's mysterious kiss is some sort of lingering stamp, a memento from her own earlier time in Neverland. That memento would surely endorse her as Mind-Tidier, nightly Neverland explorer. I am trying not to compare Mrs. Darling's kiss with a teacher's license, but the comparison is tempting.

With a detailed and individualized familiarity with her students' minds, and a likely background in the very areas of their interests, what other teaching attributes does Mrs. Darling possess? It doesn't take long, only a few pages into the substance of the play and novel, for her to show her mastery of storytelling. She first brings this skill to bear in telling her husband (himself, a somewhat childish and flustered adult) about the boy she has seen at the window, and she does so with a style and tact that renders him an open and believing listener. It is impossible to miss his shift in demeanor from being a hysterical father, brushing aside dog hair and bemoaning the way nobody respects his melodramatic urgency about the evening's plans, to that of a calm, attentive partner as he listens to Mrs. Darling's description of Peter.

Later that same night, not long into Peter's conversation with Wendy, the Darling girl asks Peter why he has come to the nursery window. Here, then, comes a reiteration of Mrs. Darling's influence: "your mother was telling you such a lovely story," Peter answers.[17] When he explains that he has to leave to go tell the Lost Boys the latest detail from "Cinderella" (the story that Mrs. Darling was telling on his most recent visit, and that Wendy has just summarized for him), Wendy eagerly volunteers her services in her mother's place as their resident storyteller. The student will become the teacher, and her students are eager for her lessons, stories that, sadly, their lives otherwise are desperately lacking.

This is one model of education portrayed in *Peter Pan*, the teacher not as a didact, but as a storyteller, and the student as the child uniquely surrendering to his or her imagination, and bracing for the complex journey into adulthood. It is in Peter's vision of that very journey where we find the first sign of a counterbalancing image of education—that which prepares children for the tedious grown-up life, a life devoid of belief, play, and imagination, and burdened with obligation. That image is portrayed most clearly and consistently (even, as Holt and Gatto would have predicted, painfully) through Captain Hook, and not because he is a brutal pirate whose greatest pleasure is the expression of power. I will not argue that Hook is analogous to an abusive teacher, but rather a perennially underserved, even abused student, having moved through an educational system that failed him.

Let's take these latter two examples in their turn. First, Peter as a drop-out. He rejects the definitions of adulthood that his parents (at least as he understands them) offer. He passes on their visions of "growing up" to move into traditional family and career, and opts instead to run away to live forever in Neverland. Periodically throughout the novel and the play, details of the formal education that promises that track present themselves as trivialities. For example, the narrator uses a debate about English grammar in order to distinguish Peter from its superficiality, as in the beginning of chapter 5 in the novel, when we learn that, "the Neverland had again woke into life. We ought to use the pluperfect and say wakened, but woke is better and was always used by Peter."[18] In this statement, the narrator draws attention to the grammar as a formality by referring to it by its technical term, and in acknowledging that the incorrect form, "is better," the narrator seems to be reinforcing the notion that storytelling outweighs a grammatical precision.

Your English teacher would take off points, the narrator seems to say, but I prefer the mistake.

Mr. Darling seems to embody the kind of adult that Peter is determined never to become. In the opening of both the play and the novel, though developed more fully in the novel, the Darlings are described as being financially strapped. Their first reaction to the birth of Wendy, their oldest, is to worry whether they can afford to feed her. They regularly refer to their one maid, Eliza, as "the servants," because the reference sounds more prosperous. They have a dog, not because they are especially fond of Newfoundlands for pets, but because that's all they can afford to fill the household role of nurse. For the social rank to which they aspire and with the children they have, a nurse they must employ. The Darlings, led by Mr. Darling, are a family who struggle to keep up the appearances required to live at the level of society to which Mr. Darling aspires. The pressure of that priority explains his frustration on the night the children left for Neverland, as he enters the nursery unable to tie his tie: "I warn you of this, mother, that unless this tie is round my neck we don't go out to dinner to-night, and if I don't go out to dinner to-night, I never go to the office again, and if I don't go to the office again, you and I starve, and our children will be flung into the streets."[19] This is the kind of "adulting" that Peter was determined never to give his parents the chance to raise him to accept. It is, however, the result of Mr. Darling's own pursuit of the generally normal goals of professional and social (and, by definition, financial) success. These are goals generally developed through promises generally made in school. It is the model of schooling that encourages the connection between hard work and traditional measures of achievement. Mr. Darling, consequently, as the product of this model, has transitioned from the dutiful student to the dutiful professional, attempting to follow every rule and complete every assignment in pursuit of the "A" he imagines in the form of promotion and status, acceptance at "the office," and a sure fire way to avoid their diametric opposite, financial destitution.

Does it work? In some respects, yes. We can see that the Darlings are at least comfortable. They have a two-story house with a backyard in a nice neighborhood (though they may not be able to afford it as fully as their more accomplished neighbors). They do have a maid (even if she is just a one person "staff" of servants) and a nurse (even though she is a Newfoundland dog). They have three children whom as yet, despite the Darling's original fears, they are managing to feed. Mr. Darling is employed in the kind of position that reflects a level of advanced education. I mean, he's not a shopkeeper or a chimney sweep; he works in an office with people who throw the kinds of dinner parties that require wearing tuxedos and evening gowns. This is the life to which Mr. Darling most likely aspired, and which his formal education has afforded him and prepared him well for. Captain Hook might have expected at least as much from his own education at Eton.

In fact, for his final spoken words in the play, Hook, "climbs the bulwarks murmuring 'Floreat Etona,' and prostrates himself into the water."[20] The phrase translates from Latin to mean something like, "May Eton always flourish!" That he expresses it marks Hook's undying (and, literally, dying) obsession with the school, and that it is murmured (not shouted or cheered) at his very lowest point as he finally has been done in by his nemesis, Pan, implies that he is still haunted by the school's effect on him. The novel offers a more detailed account of his experience as a student.

The school's "traditions still clung to him like garments," and "he still adhered in his walk to the school's distinguished slouch."[21] Put more generally, among the things that James Hook learned while at Eton were dress and walk, both superficial signs of belonging there. Another personal attribute for which he developed an obsession at Eton, and continues throughout his life to pursue and police, is the elusive and deeply valued trait, "good form." Even as Hook obsesses about good form, and he wonders, "Was it not bad form to think about good form?"[22] In this single-minded, though always slightly off point pursuit, Hood resembles the marginal student cramming for a test, only inevitably and repeatedly to discover that he has prepared for the wrong questions. In his adult life, he excels at the dress and styling. Introduced by the narrator as "never more sinister than when he was most polite,"[23] ultimately, and especially when he was alone, "there was no elation in his gait,"[24] and even in the midst of his final conflict, "his mind was no longer with [the boys swarming around him]; it was slouching in the playing fields of long ago . . . and his shoes were right, and his waistcoat was right, and his tie was right, and his socks were right."[25] All dreams of good form, and yet in his final gesture, Hook can only manage to make Peter exhibit bad form. He "made Peter kick instead of stab. . . . 'Bad form,' he cried jeeringly, and went content to the crocodile."[26]

The two versions, taken together, offer a telling portrayal of Hook's education at Eton. The play shows him "murmuring" a recognition of the school's value, and the novel shows him policing in another the very Eton value which he has never managed to achieve himself—good form. The full promise of Hook's education is that which is always just beyond his reach, always the criteria of the school and the accomplishments of his classmates ever judging him as inadequate, always the haunting force which drives him to superficial imitation instead of substantive accomplishment. It is as if Hook has gotten a passing grade by copying someone else's answers, or perhaps he is that student who read every assignment, attended every class, and followed every item on the rubric, but got a C because (says the chin-scratching teacher), "there's just something missing." Through that educational lens,

Barrie is pointing out, especially through the character of James Hook, that most formal education (driven by unachievable, arbitrary, or subjective values) sets up the most desperate students for failure.

How is Wendy's educational power as a storyteller any different from that? If there is a positive image of schooling, it really should be Wendy. First, she is the one character who is actually portrayed as a teacher, and not simply a flawed, victimized recipient of education. Consequently, a look at her work should reveal at least some particular goals for, perhaps even some noticeable outcomes of, good teaching. Second, as a teacher, Wendy offers at least two identifiable methods, and not just (as with Peter, Mr. Darling, and Captain Hook) perspectives on someone else's agenda. Third, Wendy comes with her own classroom full of students (a.k.a., The Lost Boys) whose response to her teaching can be immediately observed. Considering first the methods, I turn my attention to the passages in which Wendy is serving in the role for which she is originally recruited—storyteller.

To start with, there is evidence that the boys already have been engaged in story. Peter implies that he has been listening at the nursery window for some time now, bringing stories back to Neverland for his charges. Also, both Peter and Tootles show clear signs of understanding contrived drama (even melodrama) as it is discovered in the play that the latter has shot Wendy. When Peter asks the identity of the culprit, Tootles confesses. "Oh, dastard hand!" Peter cries, raising the arrow as if to kill Tootles, to which Tootles replies, "baring his breast, 'Strike Peter; strike true!'"[27] These are the words of readers who already are fully aware of the rhetoric and rhythm of narrative. So, perhaps Peter is the first true teacher in the story, except that Peter obviously doesn't see himself in that role, since it is he who has recruited Wendy. The dynamics are not at all different from those of a well-intended parent (in this case, portrayed as Peter) who reaches the limits of his service and sends his children to school for more advanced learning.

And so, back to Wendy. While she enters a situation in which her charges already are well-versed in imagination and the language which conveys it, she brings to this relationship her own background in the story. As I note earlier, it is her mother, Mrs. Darling, who is first the teller of stories. Mrs. Darling, not Wendy, is telling the story of Cinderella that Peter returns over and again to the window to hear. It is Wendy, however, who has studied this method from her mother, who has heard the story before, and who finishes the story when Peter asks how it ends.

In what both the play and the novel refer to as, "The Home Under the Ground," Wendy expands and personalizes her "teaching style" not simply continuing as the one who (like her mentor mother) tells stories, but as a facilitator for the children's enacting their own stories. Their actions, further, not only are instructional (they engage the children in the life roles that

Wendy is attempting to teach them), but evaluative (their performances show evidence of their genuine curiosity about and growing mastery of those life roles). In this respect, Wendy is the teacher who comes to class in costume, not only to lecture on the day's topic, but to perform it in order to engage her students more directly in their learning.

It works. The Lost Boys fall right into line with their roles as children around teacher/mother-Wendy's table. They not only seem to be playing along with Wendy as if she has introduced a new game, but also fully aware of its being make believe, fully aware that they are acting out roles. For example, though Nibs refers to her as "Mummy," John raises his hand (like any good student might) and asks, "May I sit in Peter's chair, as he is not here?" Wendy replies, "In your father's chair? Certainly not." John explains, "He's not really our father. He did not even know how to be a father till I showed up."[28] But from there, the conversation drifts back into the "story" with other boys asking for their respective roles in the drama and "complaining of" John as if he is a disruptive classmate.

The only "student" who doesn't join in comfortably is, upon his return, Peter. The Lost Boys' ring leader in imaginary games is ironically uncomfortable with the direction that Wendy's lessons take, recreating not a game of war with the Indians or pirates, but rather the warmth of home that they each have escaped. The more Wendy's work takes hold, the more the children begin thinking about their own families, and the more uncomfortable Peter is with his role as father. "It is only pretend, isn't it, that I am their father?" he asks. "Oh, yes," Wendy answers. Her line continues, "But they are ours, Peter, yours and mine." Peter replies, "But not really?" "Not if you don't wish it," Wendy says. To which Peter resolves, "I don't."[29] The line of Wendy's simulation (so to speak) has been blurred, and both teacher and student are left to negotiate the lesson, the teacher considering how far to push, and the student considering when to opt out.

In the novel, Wendy's review of outcomes leaves her less concerned about how eager her students are to believe the simulation than how disconnected they have become from what she's simulating. Put another way, one of the goals of Wendy's stories could be described as preparing the children for re-entering the lives they abandoned as much younger children. One way of accomplishing that goal is to offer them practice at role playing for the family life they may return to. One important requirement for role playing for family life is a realistic memory of that family—of real mothers, fathers, and other details of home. Thus, the stories that Wendy guide, putting the children into those roles, are Barrie's way of portraying the importance (on larger scale) of Neverland (ironically, precisely so) to growing up. If a child goes to Neverland, not to escape adulthood, but to prepare for it properly so as to arrive at adulthood with imagination and whimsy fully intact, then it is important for that child to remember the "real world" life he has left, and not to start believing that Neverland's stories are all there are. Such is a memory that Wendy finds, at times, failing, and (consequently) in need of retrieval: "What did disturb her at times was that John remembered his parents vaguely only, as people he had once known, while Michael was quite willing to believe that she was really his mother. These things scared her a little."[30]

In an effort to channel her "instruction" toward preparing her students for return, not indulge them in reveling in the stasis of remaining forever in Neverland, Wendy calls (maybe in desperation) on some more traditional teaching methods: "Nobly anxious to do her duty, she tried to fix the old life in their minds by setting them examination papers on it, as like as possible to the ones she used to do at school."[31] Even the narrator's language here connotes a serious application of tradition and structure (as may be the case when a teacher is prompted to start taking attendance or grading more rigorously). Such qualifiers as, "nobly anxious," driving forces such as, "duty," and even the goal of "fix"-ing, not relating, empowering, or imagining, all let the reader know that the lesson now needs to be taken seriously, that the teacher has given the class that look. Interestingly, the students who are the most responsive to that form of teaching are the ones for whom structure and seriousness may be most welcomed. Wendy is worried about the comments of her two brothers, and yet they have only just recently left the serious world, and only just arrived in the freedoms and games of Neverland. The Lost Boys, however, who have often half-thought about their long lost parents and the times from which they came, loved these lessons and participated with full engagement. Is it simply easier for the more seasoned residents of Neverland to consider Wendy's "tests" just one more kind of game? Or is it more likely that they found in her questions a prompting to consider something that Peter consistently discouraged—thoughts of home?

To Wendy's variety of academically phrased questions (i.e., "What was the colour of Mother's eyes? Which was taller, Father or Mother?") all of the Lost Boys responded with enthusiasm, "The only boy who replied to every question was Slightly,"[32] who also happened to the be the only boy who had entered Neverland still holding memories of his mother, the woman who had left him wrapped and tagged with the note "Slightly Soiled," thus his name.

Finally, as the narrator succinctly states, "Peter did not compete."[33]

Let's look at that moment a bit more carefully. I have already explored how Peter shunned the promises of "growing up" once (so it would seem, and for all). He shunned, likewise, the kind of learning that would lead to an adulthood toiling away in a bank or insurance office, living each day to impress some boss who might invite him (or not) to the kind of dinner party that would be more important than pausing to kiss his children good night or tidy up any of their minds. That promise, he has shunned. Meanwhile, he has become the kind of teacher in Neverland who encourages the same resistance to growing up in all of his charges, moving swiftly from one game to the next to the next, except when he happens to fall asleep and dream, "more painful than the dreams of other boys. For hours he could not be separated from these dreams, though he wailed piteously in them."[34] Using Mrs. Darling's earlier references to that special territory found in dreaming, it seems that Peter's own Neverland is fueled by his remembering arriving one night unwelcomed at his family's locked window, and finding another child sleeping in his bed. This is Peter's own recurring dream. Peter tells this story to Wendy and the Lost Boys, once, when prompted to account for his mistrust of Wendy's simulations. The simulations remind him of the reality he has escaped, but now keeps finding in dreams. Their painful memories inspire his lessons of the adventurous life in the Neverland portrayed in Barrie's fictions, free as that life is from not only the boredom of adulthood, but also the pain of childhood rejection. But since it is a Neverland badly created (not through dreams, but in order to escape the imagery found in dreams), it is one that always fails to serve Peter fully.

Those memories also shape the way Peter responds to Wendy's attempts to teach her pupils about returning to their respective childhoods and families. It is precisely as Peter reassures them that mothers "are like that," that John and Michael turn to their sister, "Let us go home." "'Yes,' she said, clutching them,"[35] and then, to the other Lost Boys, "if you will all come with me I feel almost sure I can get my father and mother to adopt you."[36] Against Peter's will and advice, the boys plead with him to let them accept Wendy's offer. The only thing at this point in the narrative that is certain is that Peter is resolved. He will not be swayed to Wendy's view of family, mothers, or growing up. As a student, he has decided (regardless of the feelings of the others) what he will learn, and what he will not. Some students are like that. As a teacher, he has decided what must be encouraged, modeled, and monitored, and what is not acceptable. Some teachers are like that.

Wendy, by contrast, can be seen as a force drawing her students back to a natural reality, the real life in a world of growing through meaningful experiences, across a lifespan.

So, what about Captain Jas. Hook as a teacher? After all, he also has "students," in the form of his crew. In that context, readers see him in the role of leader. In that role, if indeed Peter is the kind of teacher we might call inflexible, focused exclusively (even obsessively) on his particular agenda, then Hook is brutal. However, since both leave their pre-Neverland worlds with resentments, it stands to reason that both would pass the expression of that resentment along to others. There are signs of that effect for Peter in the narrative of his return from London with the Darling children. The exposition introducing Act II indicates the anxious fear all across Neverland upon

Peter's return: "everybody and everything know that they will catch it from him if they don't give satisfaction."[37] Mr. Pan's coming, Mr. Pan's coming! Everybody sit down and be quiet!! So to speak.

Similarly, what we first learn of Captain Hook in the novel is that, "as dogs this terrible man treated and addressed [his crew], and as dogs they obeyed him."[38] True to the myth of the bully, Hook shows latent signs of cowardice, "A man of indomitable courage, the only thing at which he flinches is the sight of his own blood . . . . At his public school," (remember Eton?), "they said of him that he 'bled yellow.'"[39] Such a personal history is reminiscent of the sadness that fuels Pan's anger and bravado. To emphasize the comparison, the narrator summarizes his introduction of Hook by noting, "Such is the terrible man against whom Peter Pan is pitted. Which will win?"[40] This question is echoed in the title of the novel's chapter 9, "Hook or Me This Time." It is the chapter delivering the scene of Pan's and Hook's final battle, a battle which even though Peter wins, leaves him afterward haunted in his sleep by yet another nightmare.

Thus, in literal plot terms, Pan wins, but arguably only through Hook's controlled surrender, and not without Pan's own suffering afterward. Consequently, it seems wiser to return via that finale to the narrator's question as a confirmation of the two characters' equality. As a successful storyteller, himself, Barrie creates Peter as the narrative's most obvious hero, and yet it isn't Peter's way that wins outright in the end, any more than it is Hook's, but rather Wendy's. Prepared and prompted by this teacher/mother, the children DO return to London. In spite of Peter's darker intentions, arriving ahead of the others and locking the window, it is Wendy's own teacher, Mrs. Darling, who has a uniquely personal effect on Peter, "just as if she were inside him,"[41] her authentic grief pressing him ultimately to unlock the window allowing the Darling children back into the nursery. It is Wendy who announces to her brothers, as they are still unsure now of where they are, "Oh dear! . . . it was quite time we came back,"[42] Wendy who directs them through the nursery window and into their beds so as to, "break the joyous news more gently,"[43] and Wendy who (as the novel's final chapter begins) explains about the six Lost Boys who are waiting outside to be welcomed into the family.

It is also Wendy who, as is related through that final chapter, raises her own daughter, Jane, an unmistakable hybrid of the motherly child that Wendy once was and the impish child that Peter has remained. Wendy was first drawn to Neverland with the promise of seeing mermaids and the invitation to tell stories to children. Jane "remembers" the days when her mother could fly even more vividly than does Wendy, and by the time of Peter's return, she can offer a superior rendition of Peter's crow. "Wendy was a little startled. 'My darling, how can you know?' 'I often hear it when I am sleeping,' Jane said."[44] Even though Wendy has grown old and unable to return to Neverland, the next generation of visitor there is more than ready for the journey.

In the language of educational outcomes, Jane represents the development from her grandmother's faint memory of where she received that "one kiss" on her "sweet mocking mouth," to her mother's surrendering to the temptation to try something new and magical, to Jane's full awareness of Peter and Neverland, as well as a meta-cognitive awareness of why she can go and her mother now cannot. Jane's departure isn't all that different from a scene one might expect on the child's first day of kindergarten, or the day a freshly minted high school graduate leaves home for college. Seen as a place to pass through on one's way to a healthy, empowered, aware, and imaginative adulthood, Neverland operates as a school. In that context, all of its characters are teachers. And as with traditional school itself, there are really only two ways not to approach it—as one who already is fixed in a dysfunctional model of adulthood, thus unopen to the lessons available there; or as one who wants only to be there and never to grow through those lessons and leave well-educated. The former becomes a rigid adult, and the latter a perpetual child.

So the main meaning of the *Peter Pan* narrative, as told in both Barrie's play and novel, is not, "always to be a little boy and to have fun," as Peter explains it to Wendy at their first meeting, but rather to learn enough in childhood about stories, games, and imagination so as to become the kind of grown-up that both Peter and Hook might have been willing, even wished, to become if they'd been educated more naturally and less brutally. Consequently, the main point of going to Neverland isn't to remain there forever, but rather to find it, know it, discover it within one's own dreamscape and imagination, within one's self, then leave with its kiss—the mark of the very best kind of education, a life forever after informed, enriched, and inspirited by the lessons learned in each child's Neverland, and taken out into the world and across a lifespan.

As schools go, it delivers the kind of education that even Holt, Illich, or Gatto might approve.

NOTES

1. Jean-Jacques Rousseau, *Emile, or on Education*, trans. Allan Bloom (New York: Basic Books, 1979).

2. Ivan Illich, *Deschooling Society* (New York: Harper and Row, Publishers, 1970).

3. John Holt, *How Children Learn* (New York: Merloyd Lawrence, 1983).

4. John Taylor Gatto, *Dumbing Us Down: The Hidden Curriculum of Compulsory Schooling* (Gabriola Island, BC, Canada: New Society Publishers, 2005).

5. Ivan Illich, *Deschooling Society* (New York: Harper and Row, Publishers, 1970).

6. John Holt, *How Children Learn* (New York: Merloyd Lawrence, 1983).

7. Pat Farenga, "About Growing Without Schooling," Accessed October 6, 2020. http//www.johnholtgws.com.

8. John Taylor Gatto, *Dumbing Us Down: The Hidden Curriculum of Compulsory Schooling* (Gabriola Island, BC, Canada: New Society Publishers, 2005).

9. Ibid.

10. J. M. Barrie, *Peter Pan and Other Plays* (New York: Oxford University Press, 1995), 89.

11. Ibid.

12. Ibid.

13. Ibid.

14. J. M. Barrie, *Peter Pan: Peter and Wendy, and Peter Pan in Kensington Gardens* (New York: Penguin Books, 2004), 9.

15. Ibid., 10.

16. J. M. Barrie, *Peter Pan: Peter and Wendy, and Peter Pan in Kensington Gardens* (New York: Penguin Books, 2004), 5.

17. J. M. Barrie, *Peter Pan and Other Plays* (New York: Oxford University Press, 1995), 102.

18. J. M. Barrie, *Peter Pan: Peter and Wendy, and Peter Pan in Kensington Gardens* (New York: Penguin Books, 2004), 47.

19. Ibid., 17.

20. J. M. Barrie, *Peter Pan and Other Plays* (New York: Oxford University Press, 1995), 146.

21. J. M. Barrie, *Peter Pan: Peter and Wendy, and Peter Pan in Kensington Gardens* (New York: Penguin Books, 2004), 117.

22. Ibid.

23. Ibid., 50.

24. Ibid., 117.

25. Ibid., 132.

26. Ibid.

27. J. M. Barrie, *Peter Pan and Other Plays* (New York: Oxford University Press, 1995), 113.

28. Ibid., 127.

29. Ibid., 129–130.

30. J. M. Barrie, *Peter Pan: Peter and Wendy, and Peter Pan in Kensington Gardens* (New York: Penguin Books, 2004), 70.

31. Ibid.

32. Ibid.

33. Ibid.

34. Ibid., 110.

35. Ibid., 98.

36. Ibid., 100.

37. J. M. Barrie, *Peter Pan and Other Plays* (New York: Oxford University Press, 1995), 105.

38. J. M. Barrie, *Peter Pan: Peter and Wendy, and Peter Pan in Kensington Gardens* (New York: Penguin Books, 2004), 49.

39. J. M. Barrie, *Peter Pan and Other Plays* (New York: Oxford University Press, 1995), 108.

40. J. M. Barrie, *Peter Pan: Peter and Wendy, and Peter Pan in Kensington Gardens* (New York: Penguin Books, 2004), 50.

41. Ibid., 139.

42. Ibid., 140.

43. Ibid., 141.

44. Ibid., 149.

Chapter 4

The Wind in the Willows and Plato's "Allegory of the Cave"

INTRODUCTION

When in the very opening of a novel, a frustrated yet freshly resolved character leaves behind his old routines and climbs out of a hole into the light of day, and when you're writing about that novel as study of education, it's hard not to go straight to Plato's "Allegory of the Cave."[1]

In Book VII of *The Republic*, Plato writes of a person sitting among other people, all of whom believing that what they are experiencing is simply reality, the only reality. They look at images that move before them in a light provided for them to see, and they feel confined to this location, believing that their chains prevent them from moving around, and ultimately accepting that condition without question. Then one of them, as the allegory goes, is compelled to move from his seat, upward toward a bright exit. Looking around, he realizes that the images he has been led to accept as reality are merely shadows cast on the wall, shadows of artificial figures being moved around in front of a light source. He discovers further that the light source is not natural light but cast by a fire built on a platform behind the moving figures. All he has been taught to consider real has been nothing more than a prepared and, more importantly (especially to this analysis), very limited replica of what lies ahead—another light, painfully bright at first, coming from a corridor leading upward and out of the cave. Realizing his newly acquired freedom, the person at first is forced, and then (as his eyes adjust) resolves, to pursue the source of the distant light. The closer he gets to the outside the more uncomfortable he becomes, the experience being not just new and real, but also somewhat overwhelming in its intensity.[2]

When he finally exits the tunnel and emerges from the cave, he is at first blinded by the sun's natural power, but as his eyes adjust he begins to see the beauty of the larger world, a world he has been denied during his life in the cave, a world whose inferior substitute he has been (up to then) convinced to accept as all there is to life. In his excitement, he returns to the cave to tell the others about his discovery, knowing they will appreciate his revelation and its liberation. However, they are so accepting of their life in the cave that they find the person's news to be a sign of insanity. They reject his revelation, want nothing of the liberation he offers, and the person seems to be left with a "fork in the road" sort of decision. With his newfound knowledge, he either returns to the cave to live in constant frustration with his unenlightened friends, or he leaves his past behind and returns to the world alone to face the dangers, challenges, and insights that reality offers.[3]

The educational moral of the story, of course, is that he must do neither, but rather dwell in both realms, valuing and continuing to learn the lessons of the light, but also returning periodically to share those lessons with the less enlightened (even when they don't accept those lessons), to honor the reality of one's past, and to honor those who still live in those earlier conditions.

Or, as Socrates put it, "to see the good and to go up that ascent; and, when they have gone up and seen sufficiently, not to permit them . . . to remain there and not be willing to go down again among those prisoners or share their labors and honors, whether they be slighter or more serious."[4]

What follows is an analysis of how this narrative and variations on it weave throughout Grahamme's novel. Characters in *The Wind in the Willows* occupy a variety of positions within Plato's allegory. There is the original going out. There are returns home. There are characters who live beyond the boundary of cultural comfort, yet who create home there, and those who return to civilization when circumstances call for it without feeling trapped. The departure from any analogous cave in this novel isn't consistently constructive or enlightening. That all depends on the journey out, the character making that journey, and the purpose it is designed to accomplish. Likewise, the return to any analogous cave isn't consistently a surrender by one considered crazy by those he encounters. Often as not, it is the cave itself which is elevated in status, and included among the domain of honorable, authentic life. But that takes some time and its own brand of journeying. So, let's begin.

THE READING

"The Mole was working very hard all morning, spring-cleaning his little home."[5] Kenneth Grahamme's novel opens with a Mole who has a life that is busy and productive, especially at "spring cleaning" time. Yet, Mole has become less and less proud of his work, and even of his humble home which is the target of that spring cleaning. In a positive sense, Mole's growing frustrations do not hold him back, but rather, by their contrast to what he imagines must surely lay ahead, compel him to grow. As the novel opens, he is ready (literally) to climb, to leave the darkness of his hole and explore the larger world above him. It cannot be ignored as well that the lot in life with which he begins, toiling away underground, is a lot in life specifically identified by his very nature as a mole. Biologically speaking, moles tunnel and live underground. It is an extension of who they are. For a mole to wish to live above ground could be considered unnatural, even dangerous. Here is the first connection with the conceptual debate—to aspire for growth, or to see growth as a threat to one's natural and comfortable, albeit naïve equilibrium. I mean, Mole's urges for a glimpse of the larger world are real. His emotions about facing yet another frustrating annual cleaning are equally real.

In any case, whether or not he actually grows right away, Mole does leave his underground home and emerges into the bright light of the wider world in the meadow. It is a moment that might also be compared with the character in Plato's allegory who finally realizes that he is not actually shackled to his bench in the cave and wanders out into the light of the real sun (not merely a fire built behind him) and really experiences life (away from the shadows of artificial figures marched back and forth in front of the fire).

As Mole explores that new, sunny world, he meets the Water Rat, a character who is quite settled into his own life in a home along the river. In some respects, Rat's home is also underground, as it is situated in the river bank. However, unlike the life which Mole has come to see as limited and boring, Rat's life is filled with abundance and appreciation. Rat has his routines as much as Mole does, but he fills his life with pleasure and experience, not just busy-ness and necessity. Shortly after their introductions, Rat discovers that Mole knows nothing about the river and has never been on a boat. His own passion for both prompts in Rat veritable paroxysms of revelry about just how central the river is to his life's very sense of purpose, and how much "messing about in boats" both pleases him and allows him to explore the river he loves to much: "Believe me, my young friend, there is *nothing*—absolutely nothing—half so much worth doing as simply messing about in boats."[6]

The prospect of going boating leads quickly to the prospect of packing a picnic, which introduces the next feature of Rat's love of life and material difference from his new friend, the feature of available abundance. Rat appears with his "luncheon basket":

> "What's inside it?" asked the Mole, wriggling with curiosity. "There's cold chicken inside it," replied the Rat briefly; "cold tongue cold ham cold beef pickled gherkins salad french rolls cress sandwidges potted meat ginger beer lemonade sodawater—."[7]

Rat's enthusiasm, expressed typographically through the author's unpunctuated stream of detail, is so nonjudgmental, generous, and contagious that Mole feels nothing but enthusiasm, himself, about the prospect of going out on the water with such a feast. Rat's self-deprecation shows humility, but also marks a social difference between him and the mole, answering the latter's utter amazement with the acknowledgement, "it's only what I always take on these little excursions."[8] Later, as the boat tips and the picnic basket falls overboard, Mole is upset about ruining the supplies, but Rat responds to him with an apparent awareness of and sensitivity to Mole's novice skills. He shows kindness for Mole's feelings, not anger at Mole's role in tipping the boat. Rat's response in this event shows what emerges as a pattern between Rat (as already more worldly and educated) and Mole (as one aspiring to learn) in which Rat allows Mole to make mistakes within the context of growth, then offers his support as Mole adjusts to the sting of the mistake.

In the context of the Allegory, Rat is the escapee, living richly in and out of his own hole. He has found a newly above-ground citizen and attempts to ease the newbie into above-ground life. As that newbie, Mole is only beginning to identify some of the particulars which he aims to take away from his learning enterprise. Thus, one essential difference between the two new friends is that Mole is the novice and Rat is the expert. Fueling the latter's work as teacher is Rat's empathy with (as well as hope for) Mole's struggle. Extending from that is another essential connection, Mole's own determination to join the world that Rat already occupies.

Rat even knows to warn Mole about "The Wild Wood," and more menacing still, "The Wide World," both of which he not only understands the dangers of but shows experience at navigating. However, before considering how Rat monitors Mole's curiosities about those wilder, wider ranging worlds, I want to look at the next character whom Grahamme introduces into his narrative, Mr. Toad. Toad takes abundance to the level of childish opulence, and with caution completely out of the picture he takes initiative and experience into the domain of foolhardy self-indulgence. Toad has not so much left the cave, as he treats everything as if it is his cave, his artifice, in which to revel. For Mr. Toad, adventure is an antidote for boredom, but is far from an enterprise in learning. Toad does not leave his familiar spaces to learn or to widen his awareness of the world, he does so to amuse himself unreflectively and usually at someone else's expense.

Toad's life is strewn with abandoned whims, hobbies which first occurred to him as great passions and which quickly lost their appeal as their challenges became uncomfortable, or as new "passions" displaced ones that had become boring. Boats are stacked recklessly in the boathouse as Toad announces to Rat that his next fascination is travelling the countryside in a caravan. Just as the caravan life is turning out to be a bit more rustic than Toad had bargained for, the group of travelers (Mole, Rat, and Toad) are overrun along the roadway by a motorcar. In its passing wake, however, Toad is upset less by crashing his caravan than he is smitten by the roar and speed of the car, his next indulgence. Driven (pardon the pun) by these impulses, Toad "personifies" a learner upon whom the struggle to become educated is never noticed much less reflected upon. Not only is that education not used for practical purposes, but it is hardly even used for personal enrichment or pleasure. It is merely a license which affords him (and excuses his) impulsivity, and which earns him the friendship of other educated characters often through their pity of his general helplessness, and at best by their honoring his friendship, his heart (as Socrates urges his returning escapee to do), in spite of his behavior.

Speaking of acting on impulse, back at Rat's warm and cozy home Mole has decided (against Rat's strong advice) to strike out on his own to explore the Wild Wood. He gets rather deep into the woods, and winter's darkness begins to settle in by the time Rat discovers him missing. Rat has lost track of his new friend, as it is portrayed, not simply because The Mole is a sneaky escape artist, but because Rat (when he isn't napping by his fire) is absorbed with the writing of poetry, his own thoughtful amusements though of an active more substantive and creative mind than Toad's. Much as he enjoys messing about in boats, he also enjoys messing about with verse. As he enjoys this past time, Mole continues his own more pragmatic pursuits. He wants to explore the Wild Wood, because he has a goal and the determination to accomplish it.

However, he explores without the knowledge of what the wood entails, whether its landscape of holes and caves, its flora of snarled trees and brambles, or its fauna of weasels and stoats. Nor does he know what spending the night alone there will require of him, should he lose his way (as predictably, he does). Upon waking from a fireside doze, Rat realizes that Mole is missing, intuits where he has gone, and goes out to find him. A previous draft of that sentence used the word, "rescue," in place of, "find." "Rescue," does not quite fit Rat's agenda. "Find," may not quite be it, either, but the main point is that Rat is far more interested in keeping Mole safe through his journey than he is in interrupting that journey. Rat understands the power of experience. He has, to borrow imagery from Plato's allegory, spent more time than Mole outside the cave. Consequently, he values the prospective benefits of Mole's struggle, and even of his ignorance. He just wants to help Mole survive the journey in order to reap those benefits.

Fortunately, Rat does find his friend alive, buried under a pile of leaves to protect himself from the evening's snowfall and dipping temperatures. They journey together through the forest to a place that Rat recalls but cannot precisely locate—the home of the next character along the continuum of the educational maturity, Mr. Badger. Badger is portrayed as being somewhat older than Rat. Grahamme suggests that he is more wealthy, less rustic of the two if only because he is more intellectual and reclusive, not as interested in dirtying his hands even at a potentially interesting activity as he is in minding his own business and being left alone in return. He is a "man" of manners, the manners of propriety and distance, and his education seems to have promoted this frame of mind more than the mind for poetry, boats, and picnics. He is, as well, not a "man" of whims and indulgences. Even earlier in the novel, before we meet him at his home in the Wild Wood, he appears along the riverbank and "harrumphs" when he is seen (just before quickly darting away). This "harrumphing" is not an expression of disregard for other characters, but rather a statement of his desire for privacy. He does, after all, live in The Wild Wood among all kinds of creatures who would just as soon raid and vandalize his home as not. Near the end of the novel, that's exactly what they do to Toad Hall. If education has afforded Toad his careless sense of entitlement and Rat his experiential openness, it has afforded Badger his peaceful solitude.

However, it is a solitude which he quickly and cheerfully surrenders on that winter's night after Mole stumbles over Badger's shoe scraper, hidden under the snow, and the two travelers (Rat realizing where they are) knock at Mr. Badger's door. Before meeting Badger, however, it is important to pause over this incident at his doorway. It is, as I mentioned, Mole's stumbling over Badger's scraper that leads to Rat identifying Badger's residence. However, it isn't Mole who sees his discovery for what it is, but rather Rat's recognition of what Mole's discovery implies. In fact, since Mole isn't aware of his own discovery, he complains that Rat is wasting time as the latter digs snow away from Badger's door sign. It is only when Mole sees the sign, "MR BADGER," that he credits his friend's intellectual superiority.

"You're simply wasted here, among us fellows,"[9] he cheers. In a spontaneous flourish of praise leading up to this final pronouncement, Mole's grammatically flawed, working-class language reinforces his (as yet) educational inferiority to Rat. Though his references to the contrast between books and "real life" reiterates both that he has done his homework, so to speak, and that he now is aware of the difference between artifice and reality. Rat's response to Mole's admiration seems also to acknowledge that difference quite calmly and objectively: "If only I had your head, Ratty—" Mole concludes, to which Rat answers, "But as you haven't . . . I suppose you're going to sit on the snow all night and *talk*?"[10] Another passing comment on the contrast between language and action.

Almost as an extension of that adjusting balance, Badger first greets them, murmuring his mock reprimand, "'Now the VERY next time this happens,' said a gruff and suspicious voice, 'I shall be exceedingly angry.'" Then, as soon as Rat speaks, Badger softens his voice and welcomes them in: "Come along in, both of you at once. Why, you must be perished."[11] Of course, the change in attitude may be explained by Badger's recognizing an intellectual peer, since his voice changes upon recognizing the Rat. If this is so, then he includes Mole within that recognition, inviting them both. I prefer reading his "greeting" as a requirement of his persona, and his welcome a reflection of his true personality and warmth hiding just beneath the gruff veneer. More is the proof of his generosity when he offers them not only temporary shelter from the elements, but food, a place to spend the night, and his own brand of heartfelt attention to their ultimate plan for recovering their friend Toad from the predicament he has created for himself.

If Badger were originally being polite to the two visitors because of associating Mole within the same educational rank as Rat, spending time with the Mole (not to mention, seeing that he is a mole) gives Badger every opportunity he would need to dismiss the geographically inferior animal. From the very start, however, Badger includes Mole (as did Rat) as a friend, fully and unconditionally welcomed among the emerged, regardless of how newly so. The two of them together, Rat and Badger, show Mole the practical advantages of intellectual education, as they discuss through principle and reason how to help their mutual friend, Toad. Mole is only just beginning to feel like a legitimate equal to his two new privileged and educated friends when social reality strikes on his and Rat's walk back to Rat's riverbank home the next morning. In short, Mole is called back to his "cave," and at first he is trapped between longing and (because of his recent enlightenment) shame.

The moment begins as Rat is talking with such focus as to miss Mole's request for them to stop. Mole has sensed that they are close to his own home, his old hole in the ground, once the object of his tidying and care, and then of his frustration and escape. As they walk along, Rat obliviously in the lead, Mole finally no longer can resist the call he is feeling: "'Please stop, Ratty!' pleaded the poor Mole, in anguish of heart. 'You don't understand! IT's my home, my old home! I've just come across the smell of it, and it's close by here, really quite close. And I must go to it, I must, I must! O, come back, Ratty! Please, please come back!'"[12]

In what seems to vacillate between condescension and genuine appreciation, Rat apologizes for ignoring Mole's request for them to stop, then compliments Mole's humble home as they find it. Meanwhile, Mole's emotional arc follows nearly the opposite course, beginning as a defiant, then plaintive insistence on stopping to honor properly his deeply and suddenly felt sense of home, then descending (literally and figuratively) into embarrassment at how shabby and simple that home is when compared with those of Rat and Badger.

However, Mole has indeed asked for what he wants, and Rat honors him, appreciates him, without pity or condescension. At this point in the novel,

Mole, Rat, and Badger have formed a community of equals, each reflecting a set of values and mental life that complements their mutual friendship, with one (Mole) being especially simple, open, and pragmatic, and another (Badger) being especially aloof, reflective, and resolved. Another force that holds them together—and this becomes a narrative emphasis driving much of the remainder of the novel—is their common determination to save their friend (challenging though he may be), Mr. Toad.

The last time I mentioned him, Toad had become enamored with automobiles, and by extension with accumulating and then wrecking them. Consequently, his friends, Mole, Rat, and Badger have planned what in modern times would be called an intervention. Knowing about not only Toad's recent and dangerous obsession with cars, but also his generally impulsive nature, they call Toad in for a meeting whereby they intend to confront him with the hazards of his ways and, in providing such a confrontation, to give him the insights required to mend those ways. In this scene, they are not all that different from the teacher, parent, principal gathering, presenting the delinquent student with a list of ways in which to reform so as to avoid dropping (or flunking) out of school. While that student is receiving his or her reprimands, he or she is often sulking, looking at the floor, often promising to comply if only to get those in authority off his or her back. Put another way, he has, perhaps long risen from the cave only to ignore the natural world around him (thus, as I suggested earlier, turning the "real world" into simply another cave), then returned to the cave more fascinated with the fire and figures down below than wary of their artifice. Perhaps as likely, he is one of those remaining in the cave, deaf to the explanations of anyone who returns from the world above.

In any case, he is neither interested in soaking up real life's lessons, nor in passing any enlightenment along to those less fortunate. As such, Mr. Toad listens to his friends and promises to reform, but only until Badger announces that reform to the others. Hearing his promise made real in that announcement, Toad simply can't resist the urge to escape his "detention," and is willing to lie outright to Rat in order to make that escape. Thus, while Rat is on watch and Badger and Mole are taking a break, Toad feigns sickness and asks for a doctor and a lawyer, and Rat (acting on an innocent, even noble and principled degree of trust) goes into town to fetch that help. Toad is far more experienced at getting out of jams (or running away from them) than he is at avoiding them ahead of time. The "intervention" so to speak, is only the first of a narrative series of his jams during this segment of the novel. Escaping his friends while Rat is away, Toad rides off in a stolen car, which he wrecks (and why would he not, since his lack of knowledge of driving equals his lack of knowledge of self-control). Wrecking, he is arrested by the police, convicted in court, and hauled off to jail, wherein one breath-catching stretch of the plot he has an opportunity to feel sorry for himself, if not to reflect on his role in his own fate.

During that brief respite from his own chaos, it doesn't take very long for Toad to create another series of mishaps, all as a plot to free himself from the mess his self-indulgent behavior already has gotten him into. He manipulates the "gaoler's" daughter, "a pleasant wench and good hearted," who comes to his cell to bring him his nightly meal and a bit of cheer.[13] One evening, the daughter is accompanied by her aunt, a washerwoman, who offers Toad her garments as a disguise. Toad walks out of jail dressed as a washerwoman, using that same ruse to catch a ride on a nearby train. The train carries him quite some distance before the fireman discovers that this washerwoman he has taken on board is none other than a loud and irritating Toad.

Let's review. Toad's impulsiveness leads him to be escape his friends, steal and wreck a car, be thrown in jail, take advantage of a virtuous jail worker, and impersonate a member of the opposite sex and the working class, thereby dismissing, exploiting, and consequently disrespecting both. Each of these turns is a reaction to situations his impulsiveness has created, none of which leads him to reflect on that behavior, much less change that behavior. Furthermore, the deeper his reactions carry him the more abusive and disrespectful he becomes, first to his peers, then to the various officers of the law, and finally to those he perceives as his social inferiors—women, laborers, and (the combo-pack) women laborers. How does he get out of this predicament, and (more important to this chapter) what does his experience say about education?

The answer to the first question is simple: luck. To escape being caught by the workers on the train, Toad leaps off the moving car. From there, he works his way through brush and bramble to the river, where his floating happens to land him directly at Rat's front door. As for the second question, what does Toad's experience say about education? That question has a two-part answer. One relates to the nature of his own education, which (as I already have claimed) seems little more than a credential of affluence. With his level of social status, during the time in which the story is set, Toad almost certainly would have "attended" a reputable public school (in English terms) and the proper college at either Oxford or Cambridge. Those advantages are extensions of his wealth and property. Rat openly and matter-of-factly acknowledges Toad's wealth. However, Rat also qualifies his description, implying that even with Toad's privileges he has a whole set of normalizing (humanizing?) flaws: "he's not a millionaire. And he's a hopelessly bad driver, and quite regardless of law and order. Killed or ruined—it's got to be one of the two things, sooner or later."[14] Toad has inherited his entire way of life, not developed it as an extension of learning from either books or experience. Not from climbing out, but also not from staying put, but rather from having what appears to be a lifetime (to this point, at least) of squandered opportunities to become enlightened through experience. He is, nevertheless, their friend, and as such Rat, Badger, and now Mole feel a duty to help, even possibly educate him.

Toad responds even less well to "lecture" than to experience. Toad will not be taught simply by being told. No amount of explanation or confrontation provided by Badger, even behind the closed doors of their private conference, will produce the outcomes of changed behavior as long as Toad's lived experience is corrupted by a combination of self-interest, impulsiveness, and a savvy avoidance of (or escape from) consequences. More simply put, as long as it's more fun to be bad than to be smart, Toad will be bad. However, this binary between smart and fun suggests a larger, binary myth about educational outcomes: a debate between the joys and burdens of staying home (applying practical life skills toward a meaningful vocation, though at the cost of cultural capital and prestige), and advantages and disappointments of going out (pursuing grand and laudatory goals, while losing touch with community and origins). Staying home (even, in the cave) vs. going out is the balance that I want now to examine more carefully across Mole, Rat, Badger, and Toad.

The novel actually opens with the going out of Mole. That much, we have covered, including the effects of that going out on his coming back with greater appreciation, albeit at first through the eyes of the visitor, Rat. Going out is also a clear educational end for Mr. Badger. He lives in the Wild Wood. True, he regularly visits the River Bank, and he is friends with both Toad and Rat (and, by association, with Mole), but he lives happily unafraid away from their general society, closer in proximity to the Stoats and Weasels of the Wild Wood (and presumably, to daily reflections of his own privacy). In fact, Badger has both feet, or perhaps rather, paws, firmly planted in "going out," as he lives in the Wild Wood (the novel's most recurring symbol of "out") and also regularly leaves his home in that outsider realm to visit the River Bank, which relative to his home, is Badger's true "out." But what about Rat? Of course, there are his regular excursions down the river in his boat, but as an extension of his familiar and beloved life on the river, that hardly feels like out. Those excursions serve more to identify the entire river as his "staying home." To find Rat's "going out," we have to look at the particular chapter devoted precisely to his wandering spirit, a chapter titled, "Wayfarer's All."

It begins, "The Water Rat was restless, and he did not exactly know why." In the chapter's opening scenes, Rat first notices a change in season and then watches as various flocks of birds begin their annual migration south to warmer climates. This observation leads him to stop a few of the birds to ask them why they are leaving and to implore at least one to stay. Yet, further reflection brings Rat to the thought that perhaps there is little reason for anyone to stay: "'Why do you ever come back, then, at all?' he demanded of the swallows jealously. 'What do you find to attract you in this poor drab little country?'"[15] It sounds a lot like Mole in his early frustrations with his boring former life, and it signals for Rat, as it did for Mole, the rising desire to go out. It also explains why one who has left the cave might be encouraged by Socrates to return periodically to it, in order to maintain contact with those still there who may not be entirely settled with that condition.

Rat reflects "restlessly" (the narrator says) as he hikes across the countryside, until he hears footsteps coming along the path nearby. It is a Sea Rat, "the wayfarer," journeying from Constantinople on his way to his most recent stop, a family farm where he plans to live for a while. The Sea Rat identifies with Rat right away. His first comments to Rat are in praise of his riverside life, "a goodly life you lead, friend; no doubt the best in the world, if only you are strong enough to lead it!"[16] Rat, however, questioning the value of that very life, refers to the plot of land where the Sea Rat is going, "his dull inland farm, about which [Rat] desired to hear nothing."[17] After beginning with a celebration of the river life he is now pursuing, the Sea Rat regales the Water Rat with stories of his world travels, including his new interest in leaving his farm and continuing along his journeying. He invites Ratty to join him, rising as he does so to continue along the path. "His voice died away and ceased, as an insect's tiny trumpet dwindles swiftly into silence; and the Water Rat, paralyzed and staring, saw at last but a distant speck on the white surface of the road," leaving the reader to wonder whether the entire encounter had been real, or simply a fantasy of Rat's momentary desire to go out into the larger world.[18]

Rat emerges from his trance when he is approached along the path by his friend, Mole. Through his conversation, Mole reminds Rat of all that is good about the world along the river. Then, in a gesture that both re-connects Rat with his own creative force and reminds readers of Rat's scholarly role, Mole brought his friend some writing paper and reminded him that, "It's quite a long time since you did any poetry."[19] Recapturing his appreciation, and his means of thinking and expressing, recapturing his sense of what is real and good, Rat is brought back from his thoughts of "going out" to what might only be its own cave-like trip, an artificial journey along someone else's path, into someone else's truth. Now, Mole has returned Rat's earlier favor (or lesson). He offers eyes through which Rat may appreciate the river bank he might have left for grander dreams of adventure, just as Rat helped Mole see simple warmth in the humble home he'd once abandoned, blinded then mere by its familiarity. Mole's full arrival as Rat's and Badger's equal is most clearly portrayed in the novel's finale, the battle to liberate Toad Hall.

It is Mr. Toad's one truly authentic "inside," one that no matter how far he travels, he is determined to return to defend, which he does after being rescued by Mole, Rat, and Badger. His friends have discovered that, in Toad's absence, Toad Hall has been occupied and ransacked by a host of weasels and stoats, and it becomes Toad's true mission to recover it from the wild beasts. It's worth mentioning that even this desperate quest comes only after an extended period of Toad's own neglect of the mansion, as his other whims have cluttered up the grounds and boathouse. Toad still lacks general respect for his family's property, but when that property is threatened from the "outside," he generates authentic respect at least for its history and meaning.

Unfortunately, even though the narrative allows Toad some claim on a reliable passion for authentic space, he still lacks any sense of strategy to prepare for the assault to reclaim his space. That work goes to the humble Mole, who has gone to Toad Hall in the once discarded disguise of the washerwoman. Mole provides the weasel guards with false information about the impending attack, a feat which puts him first in line when Badger leads the charge. In that final charge, it is less love of property than "injured pride" that motivates Toad's determination to engage in battle.[20] Then, when all is over, it is Badger (not Toad) who proposes a plan to clean up the bedrooms and clear out any of the weasels remaining upstairs. Then, it is Mole (not Rat) that Badger sends up to do that job, explaining that he'd include Rat, "if he wasn't a poet."[21] Apparently, well-educated poets aren't fit for house cleaning or clearing out riff-raff. Finally, however, it is Mole (not Rat or Badger or Toad) who comes back from his assignment having befriended the remaining weasels: "They were very penitent, and said they were extremely sorry for what they had done."[22] Mole not only cleans the rooms but also prepares them for his new guests, inviting them all downstairs for a proper dinner.

This is Mole's second display not only of intelligence but also of tact and character. His home reclaimed, Toad neither recognizes nor understands any of Mole's operation, and is actually jealous of the attention Mole is receiving for his accomplishments. Rat is distracted and happily detached. Badger is proud, fully recognizing Mole's work and value. In the end, even of Toad's going out and coming home, it is Toad who remains the most outside of the moment, captivated as he is by his own image and need for attention. By contrast, it is Mole who makes the most realistic use of Toad Hall, first as a strategist for its recovery, and then as a negotiator of the peace which follows, a peace which presumably extends at least for the moment into the Wild Wood (where his new weasel friends live). And why would that not be so, Toad Hall standing tall and opulent as perhaps the very most "outside" contrast with Mole's subterranean origin.

Working from the two extremes of the continuum, it's probably safe to say that Toad is the character who benefits the least from whatever formal education he may have had, and from the looks of his property and buying power, his is the education which most likely cost the most. It is also safe to say that Mole has both learned the most, takes his learning the farthest, and applies his learning to the most practical, experiential outcomes. His is an education which basically costs nothing except for his own courage, initiative, and adaptability. It is an extension not of his social status or bank account, but rather his hunger for growth, his openness to new experience, and his growing trust in himself. By the end of the novel, he is a far cry from the Mole who capsized the boat or got lost in the Wild Wood, much less the Mole who was stuck in his underground rut of spring cleaning. Meanwhile, Toad is almost entirely unchanged. Apart from his rallying with believable integrity to defend his home, Toad's final gesture is a performance to empty chairs in an empty room, long after the others think they have convinced him to stop showing off and to settle down.

But I did say, "almost entirely," as when he does enter the room for the banquet and is greeted warmly by the guests gathered there, Toad is genuinely struck both by the work that his friends have put into the party, and by the appreciation they are expressing for him. In that moment, when he is asked for a speech and a song, he turns modest. "He was indeed an altered Toad!" the narrator assures his reader.[23] I am not convinced, for he was an altered Toad after discarding each previous obsession, and after winding up on the run from the police, and after feeling the support of his friends who wanted to help him recover his family home. What does seem constant is others' care for Toad. What also seems constant is Toad's discomfort with real expressions of that care in return. He routinely favors (appears happier with) the world of his own playful, if not sometimes childish and manipulative creation. Toad's privilege renders him a perpetual outsider, and most of the time he thoroughly enjoys that status.

An informative contrast to that image would be the character of Badger. Badger's outsider-ness renders him energized and willing, even duty bound, when called upon to move into "society" to be of help and of service. That same outsider-ness offers him the kind of distance from those he helps to see their world through the lenses of guiding principles, conceptual and cultural wisdom, and long-developed courtesies and manners. From his home in the woods, he sees the river bank holistically, objectively, as a system of beings, while not of those beings.

Meanwhile, Rat engages his students (or at least Mole) in field trips and meals, and he comes out to find you when you drift away (thereby teaching you to come find him when he does likewise). He is kind when you need help or when you make a mistake, even though he admits to his own exasperation at your more impulsive or careless deficiencies. His education is a seamless extension of his daily reflective and appreciative engagement with the world, and he uses it not just for vocational purposes, but also, and with just as much relevance, to live an enriched life.

So as *The Wind in the Willows* shows, the citizen who decides to have a meaningful life in the cozy comforts of his or her home town can truly make a difference in the lives of those who may start out with fewer of those comforts, or who may need to find the comforts they have become unable to appreciate. Also, those who choose to leave the familiar to pursue a more exotic life can find ways to bring that life to bear on every day and humane problems. By contrast, the novel also shows that even in leaving the familiar to pursue some of life's most exotic experiences, some people fail to find the wisdom that they might otherwise bring back to their (or any other) community. Education, it would seem, depends on genuine curiosity and attentive, reasoned experience, and is functioning at its best when it simultaneously challenges and enlightens the student, and empowers the student contribute to the lives of others. In Grahamme's fictional universe as well as Plato's *Republic*, education is a sun whose true warmth anyone can find through a burst of resolve, a rigorous amount of climbing, and the ability to welcome the strangeness and mystery found in the sudden and unfamiliar brightness. It is, likewise, a responsibility that anyone can apply well with a healthy commitment to friendship and community.

NOTES

1. Plato, *The Republic of Plato*, trans. Allan Bloom (New York: Basic Books, 1968), 193–196.
2. Ibid.
3. Ibid.
4. Ibid., 198.
5. Kenneth Grahamme, *The Wind in the Willows* (London: Puffin Books, 1994), 2.
6. Ibid., 6.
7. Ibid., 7.
8. Ibid.
9. Ibid., 54.
10. Ibid.
11. Ibid., 56.
12. Ibid., 79.
13. Ibid., 132.
14. Ibid., 60.
15. Ibid., 157.
16. Ibid., 159.
17. Ibid., 166.
18. Ibid., 169–170.
19. Ibid., 172.
20. Ibid., 228.

21. Ibid., 230.
22. Ibid., 231.
23. Ibid., 241.

Chapter 5

A Bear of Very Little Brain

Winnie-the-Pooh and Growth Mindset

INTRODUCTION

Two of Winnie-the-Pooh's most iconic catchphrases are, "Oh, bother," and, as he taps his head, "Think, think, think!" Granted, the latter of those is an invention of Walt Disney; Milne's narrator simply comments that the bear "put his head between his paws and began to think."[1] However, both statements reflect anything but "a bear of very little brain." A more careful examination of his reasoning processes from one story to the next suggests that Winnie-the-Pooh is, instead, a bear of very little mental rigidity, a bear of very little arrogance or closed-mindedness, and (for those reasons) a bear of very great brain when it comes to encountering and growing through unfamiliar experiences.

At least three popular psychologists recently have articulated mental states ideal for learning. The most familiar maybe Carol Dweck's extensively researched and popular notion of "growth mindset."[2] Angela Duckworth refers to a similar cognitive trait as "grit,"[3] and Anders Ericcson identifies a related pattern across highly successful people, a behavior he refers to as "deliberate practice."[4] Dweck's theory of growth vs. fixed mindset articulates two forms of self-definition, or views of the self. Under the terms of one definition, the self is made up of fixed attributes, such as intelligence, talent, interest, or skill level. Under that definition, highly successful performance is the result of giftedness. Good grades or test scores are the result of intelligence, maybe even genius. Consequently, finding that something does not come naturally or easily is most likely a sign that one is "not good" at that thing, and furthermore that one will never be good at that thing, by virtue of not already possessing the gift or aptitude for it.[5]

Under the terms of the other definition, the self is an environment of limitless potential. One is not naturally simply gifted at one thing and not another, nor is one stuck at any given level of performance by virtue of inescapable, innate personal traits. One's performance rather occurs on a continuum, with growth fueled by the way in which one sets and perceives goals, reflects on effort and error, and practices an enterprise with the intention of improvement. This frame of mind is what Dweck calls a "growth mindset."[6]

If Dweck's work articulates the model for growth, then Duckworth's articulates the attitude that promotes it, an attitude that she refers to as "grit." The simplest description of grit is the knack for continuing to participate in an activity even after, because of the activity's difficulty, continued participation has become uncomfortable.[7] Grit is persistence. In the context of learning and developing performance, it is persistence on one's challenging way to improved, even masterful performance. To exercise grit, however, is to postpone the expectation or measurement of mastery, and attend to the feedback being provided in the sloppiness of current practice. Grit is the capacity of staying in the moment, even when the moment stops being fun, but as the moment may become especially informative.[8]

Finally, Ericcson's research and theories about learning provide Dweck's model and Duckworth's attitude with a strategy, one he refers to as "deliberate practice."[9] Deliberate practice, Ericcson explains (and observes repeatedly throughout his research on various examples of high achievement), is the mechanism which connects behavior with growth. As a musician friend once told me, "Practice makes perfect is a myth and a mistake. Practice doesn't make perfect. Practice makes permanent. PERFECT practice makes perfect." Ericcson wouldn't necessarily insist that practice has to be perfect, but he would insist that for it to lead to growth that it has to be informed, strategic, reflected upon and modified as needed, and implemented consciously.[10] Thus, with a growth mindset even about deliberate practice, one might achieve performance levels which may have defied any earlier definitions of fixed traits.

I'm not sure just how deliberate Winnie-the-Pooh is, and I'm certainly not preparing to argue that he is consciously going out into each day with a plan to grow (unless it's around his belly), but his attitude about things with which he is unfamiliar is deceptively similar to the attitude of "grit" that fuels and informs "deliberate practice," and it reflects through his assumption of not-knowing, the very perspective on progress that characterizes what Dweck advocates as "growth mindset."

THE READING

Certain, himself, that he is a bear of very little brain by not counting on raw, fixed intelligence to help him, Pooh Bear continually is open to opportunities to experience, reason, think and re-think, to try, and try differently, to ask and ask again. With each question, and especially with each open posture to the answers, he learns how to seek solutions, solve problems, and comfortably encounter new ones. Along the way, he is able to help his friends, especially when they seem already to know what's going on or what must be done. To illustrate this point, I will begin with a few observations of Pooh's approach to problem-solving as they appear in the very first story, "We Are Introduced to Winnie-the-Pooh and Some Bees, and the Stories Begin." The next three stories will be considered in order, "Pooh Goes Visiting," "Pooh and Piglet Hunt," and "Eeyore Loses a Tail." After establishing something of a baseline for Pooh's growth mindset, I will compare his approach to life with those of a few of his more cognitively fixed friends, Rabbit, Owl, Piglet, Kanga, Eeyore, and Tigger.

For starters, the very first narrated action of Pooh Bear comes in response to his hearing "a loud buzzing noise" coming from a tree in the middle of the forest. Upon hearing the noise, he, "put his head between his paws and began to think."[11] What results from his thinking isn't an answer, but rather a reasoning process. He listens, noting that the noise, "means something." He knows that it means "something," but not YET what that something is. Furthermore, he knows that it means something, because of reasoning: "You don't get a buzzing-noise like that," he says to himself, "without its meaning something."[12] The next step in his thinking is to identify the buzzing as the product necessarily of some agency. He deduces that somebody must be making the noise, and that "the only reason for making a buzzing noise that *I* know of is because you're a bee."[13] The italics in that statement are Milne's, and so by extension Pooh's, not mine. Which is to say, Milne is portraying Pooh as owning his thought process, as possibly different from someone else's, or from some absolute fact or truth. By connecting his conclusion to his perspective, or rather what he "knows of," Pooh is admitting that knowledge is both relative and malleable.

His process continues as he connects the noise's source, bees, with the product that comes from bees, honey. Then, he personalizes the purpose of honey as only Pooh might do, concluding that, "the only reason for making honey is so *I* can eat it."[14] The italics again, are Pooh's, and they function rhetorically to authorize Pooh to act on climbing the tree to retrieve the honey, even though that may not be the response that anyone else may opt for. It is, for Pooh, the conclusion of his own reasoning and the solution upon which he uniquely lands. Maybe not *the* answer, but very clearly HIS answer. That distinction becomes important because of the way it also grants him ownership over the problem and encourages further modifications as his plan unfolds. First, he falls from the tree and into a gorse bush. Then, once free from the bush, "he . . . *began to think again*."[15] The italics are mine, this time. Upon his first attempt at implementing his plan, Pooh failed, but he didn't give up. He thought. And after giving the matter some more thought, "the first person he thought of was Christopher Robin."[16] Of course, one can argue that seeking help is a form of giving up, but Pooh doesn't seek out Christopher Robin so the child could solve his problem for him. Pooh seeks out the boy as a supply source for implementing his own solution(s).

Pooh asks Christopher Robin for a balloon, already apparently developing another method for getting up to the bees' nest. When Christopher presents two different balloons, one green and one blue, Pooh holds off on determining which is the right one as he weighs their relative effects. He talks through his options, noting that with the green balloon, "they might think you were only part of the tree . . . ," and with the blue balloon, "they might think you were only part of the sky, and not notice you, and the question is: Which is most likely?"[17] When Christopher Robin points out a flaw in Pooh's plan—that the bees, in either case, would notice the Bear underneath the balloon—Pooh calmly adds that information to his considerations, determining that he will darken himself with mud and "try to look like a small black cloud." Not *look* like one, mind you, *try* to look like one. Always a work in progress. Because, as Pooh Bear acknowledges, "You can never tell with bees."[18]

Once Pooh decides to attempt to deceive the bees by looking like a cloud, the blue balloon emerges as the better option, not because it is inherently a better color, but that as a sky color it works better logically than the green one with Pooh's plan for disguising himself as a cloud. It's all quite sensible and carefully reasoned out, the result of a mind continually open to incoming data and the merits of a better idea. And at first, the plan works. Pooh does float up into the tree, muddied to appear as dark as a rain cloud. The one thing that Pooh hasn't accounted for was that the bees wouldn't be deceived. Noticing that the bees may be onto his trick, Pooh seems to attribute the same kind of reasoning process that he is using, himself. "Perhaps they think that you're after their honey," Christopher Robin says, to which Pooh replies openly, nonjudgmentally, "It may be that. You never can tell with bees."[19]

But Pooh is not ready yet to give up on his plan. Instead, he considers one more modification—that perhaps if Christopher Robin walks around under the tree with an umbrella saying, "Tut-tut, it looks like rain," the bees may take in that data as well, and reconsider Pooh's appearance as a cloud. When even this modification fails, and the bees become still more aggressive, Pooh only then decides, "I have just been thinking, and I have come to a very important decision. *These are the wrong sort of bees.*"[20] This announcement seems to have a trait of finality that earlier thoughts lack, but it is the product of continued thinking, and it leads to the same sort of reasoned exit of the plan as earlier reason led into it. It also implies that he's holding out hope for finding the right sort of bees. Even more specifically, Pooh determines not just that *these* bees are wrong, but also that the wrong sort of bees, by logical extension, "would make the wrong sort of honey."[21]

Even, once they agree that the pursuit of honey will not succeed, the plan to get Pooh down reflects one final example of the bear's resistance to absolute (or fixed) knowledge. Deciding that the best approach would be for Christopher Robin to bring Pooh down by shooting the balloon with his pop gun, Christopher's first effort is a bit off the mark:

> "*Ow!*" said Pooh.
> "Did I miss?" you asked. [The "you" is the boy, as addressed in the story by the narrator.]
> "You didn't exactly miss," said Pooh, "but you missed the *balloon.*"[22]

In other words, try again, which Christopher Robin does, hitting the balloon this time, and bringing his friend softly to the ground. By all objective measures, the whole enterprise is a failure. The deception fails to fool the bees, and the bear fails to get any honey. And yet, each step in pursuing the objective is executed reasonably, reviewed openly and honestly, and responded to intelligently. By the end, Pooh has successfully (at least in his mind) identified the kind of bees who do NOT produce the right honey.

In the next story, equally iconic in the collection's popular tradition, Pooh goes to visit Rabbit, eats all of *his* honey, and grows so large around the middle that he can't climb back out through Rabbit's front door. Similar to his approach to "the wrong sorts of bees," Pooh begins his visit by carefully evaluating the scene for its promise of honey. Though one might expect that a bee hive would be far more likely to have honey than a rabbit's den, Pooh uses the same observational inquiry that led him to abandon the bees to persist with his friend, Rabbit, until the latter offers him every morsel of honey he has. That concludes, before the main part of the story even begins, the first example of Pooh's grit in this tale. The second example is one that Pooh needs a bit of encouragement to express, the grit that allows him to accept his overgrown state, his being stuck in Rabbit's door, and Christopher Robin's proposal of the best workable solution: "We shall have to wait for you to get thin again."[23] This plan is considered as superior to the one where they simply pull the bear before he is ready, or push him back into Rabbit's house which is rejected because of Rabbit's resistance to the long-term company. Or as the rabbit more tactfully put it, "having got so far, it seems a pity to waste it."[24] In terms of grit, that is simply another way to say, why lose the ground you've gained? Likewise, why rush a process that simply needs a bit of patience?

Pooh, however, doesn't like the prospect of being patient until he can move ahead further. "I can't stay here for a week," he complains. Christopher Robin answers him with a simple dose of reality, "You can stay here all right, silly old Bear, it's getting you out which is so difficult."[25] From this point, Pooh accepts the challenge of waiting. Likewise, rather than continuing to debate other plans, the animals and the boy gathered around propose various methods for helping Pooh implement the plan they've chosen. They can visit him, read to him, Rabbit can use Pooh's hind legs as a towel-horse so that even he might endure this situation with less inconvenience. Eventually, and with the help of both Pooh's own patience and the collective tugging assistance of the entire community of animals, not to mention no small degree of pain and discomfort in the effort, the Bear pops free from the opening.

After such an ordeal, some may vow never again to get into such a "tight spot," having learned a sort of fixed message about openness and experience. Pooh, however, "with a nod of thanks to his friends . . . went on with his walk through the forest, humming proudly to himself."[26] This ending, of course, could indicate that Pooh hasn't learned anything from getting stuck. I prefer to imagine he hasn't learned to stop exploring the forest just because of one, now-happily-resolved problem.

In "Chapter III" of *Winnie-the-Pooh*, Pooh and Piglet believe they are tracking a Woozle. In fact, they become increasingly certain that the Woozles they are tracking are growing in number as they go. In reality, Pooh and Piglet are walking in a circle, tracking themselves as their footprints multiply with every lap. Granted, it isn't easy to see this behavior as the result of intelligence, until one notices the attentive degree of deductive reasoning that Pooh and Piglet exert in interpreting the multiplying tracks, given that the only scenario they don't consider is that they are walking in a circle. At no point do they abandon the task from boredom at not yet succeeding, but also at no point do they abandon it because they are afraid of the Woozle they might find at the end of the trail, even as they begin to believe that there is more than one beast who will be waiting for them there. No, they continue on, presumably more interested in encountering a Woozle than afraid of what it may do to them.

Even as the Woozles appear to be multiplying, and Piglet makes excuses for leaving to tend to some chores, Pooh calmly replies, "We'll do it this afternoon, and I'll come with you."[27] He accepts Piglet's excuses, but not his fear. He promises to help him, but challenges him to stick with their task. And even as Christopher Robin offers him a final evaluation that would appear on anyone's list of "fixed mindset" comments ("You're the Best Bear in All the World"), Pooh answers, "Am I?" posing the question rather than accepting the simple, fixed state.[28] Of course, he is happy with Christopher's words, but his reply reveals that "Best Bear" state as an object for reflection, not a state of achievement.

In the next chapter, "In Which Eeyore Loses a Tail and Pooh Finds One," it is Pooh, through his simple powers of observation, who first notices that Eeyore has lost his tail. Eeyore's first reaction is to blame someone else for having taken it, but Pooh's first reaction is to suggest the possibility that it was Eeyore who simply misplaced it—an honest and survivable error. Though this sounds like a minor distinction, it suggests a significant difference in agency and consequence. If someone has stolen Eeyore's tail, he is more likely to feel victimized and therefore helpless. If losing it is shameful, he is likely to deflect responsibility. However, if Eeyore, himself has left it somewhere, there is more of a chance he can retrace his steps and find it, and the statement itself has embedded within it the kind of responsibility that would encourage that search. And searching is precisely what Pooh sets off to do, which is what he is doing when he wanders up to the house of his friend, Owl.

Owl knows immediately how to find the missing tail (or acts as if he does). Yet, even as he begins to state the list of steps that must be observed, Owl's lofty language—"First," he says, "*Issue* a Reward"—is met with confusion by Pooh's in-the-moment attention.[29] Pooh, unfamiliar with such language as is used by one as intelligent as Owl, misunderstands the term "issue" for a sneeze, and challenges the bird to clarify himself without sneezing while he's talking. This request for clarification, a confusion between what is essentially orated with what is attentively heard, causes Owl, likewise, to be confused, not realizing the difference between what he has been taught to say, and what a practical-minded listener might understand. Owl is relying on formality, and Pooh is trying to understand and implement a method for solving a problem. As their conversation continues, "Owl went on and on, using longer and longer words, until at last he came back to where he started."[30] Not entirely clear about what kind of note should be written, Owl recalls that Christopher Robin has written all of the notes around Owl's front door. He takes Pooh out to show him those notes, each a statement offered as his own that he didn't, himself, compose (a product without process, if you will), and while they are standing by the door, Pooh sees Owl's "bell rope," which in fact is Eeyore's missing tail.

Certain it is a bell rope even from the moment he sees it draped across a bush, and after pulling it there until it came off in his hand, and assuming then that nobody wants it, Owl has brought it home to use as his own bell rope, never considering, much less recognizing through simple observation, that it not at all a bell rope, but rather Eeyore's tail. Pooh, however, makes that observation right away, and informs Owl, "you made a mistake. Somebody did want it."[31] It is a mistake that leads to immediate action, as "with these words he unhooked it and carried it back to Eeyore."[32] The chapter ends with Pooh feeling very proud of himself and celebrating with a song, the last line of which is, "*I* found the Tail!"[33] Very little brain, indeed!

I will offer one more example of Pooh's growth mindset, before turning my attention to the characters who clarify that mindset by variously fixed contrast. This last example considers Pooh's growth through a look at what may be the most popular story from Milne's entire collection, the chapter entitled, "In Which Piglet is Entirely Surrounded by Water." This story mainly offers a study in problem-solving, once again contrasting Pooh's growth to that of Piglet fixedness. After several days of rain, and with flood waters rising higher and higher, Piglet's first response is to panic, then to list all of his friends whose skills are greater than his. Through this sequence, Piglet's fixed view stands out in even clearer relief than it appears in the Woozle hunt. In naming his friend's skills, Piglet is attempting to highlight his deficiencies and thereby justify his own feelings of helplessness. It's a very trait-oriented awareness. Christopher Robin and Pooh can climb trees, Kanga can jump and Rabbit can burrow, Owl can fly, and even Eeyore has the gift of braying noisily until someone hears and rescues him. Everyone who is capable of escape thinks Piglet has a gift. All Piglet can do is wait, and he has that option only as an extension of his lack of specified attributes. Finally, he sends out a call for help, a message in a bottle. He doesn't even figure that plan out for himself, but rather remembers hearing about that sort of solution once in a story told to him by Christopher Robin. Piglet decides to write his own message, cork it up inside a bottle, toss the bottle into the rising floodwaters, and wait for help to arrive.

Meanwhile, Pooh sleeps right through the first part of the storm. He has slept so soundly because he is tired from his most recent "expotition." Earlier, after discovering "the North Pole" in another chapter, Pooh "was so proud . . . that he asked Christopher Robin if there were any other Poles such as a Bear of Little Brain might discover."[34] First, just asking the question about additional opportunities shows a mind for growth. Furthermore, when the boy mentions the South Pole, and adds, "I expect there's an East Pole and a West Pole," as well, Pooh decides on exploring the East Pole.[35] In a way it's nonsense, but seen from the perspective of learning, it reflects Pooh's sense of the possible, not the closed and absolute. Finding no one to explore the East Pole with him, Pooh sets out by himself, and returns so exhausted that he goes into a deep sleep. As he slept, he dreamed, dreamed all about life on the East Pole, which was the state of mind he was in when he was awakened by the sensation of water around his legs.

So, unlike his friend Piglet, who entered into the problem-solving process with fear and self-doubt, Pooh entered it in the middle of a dream about adventure and discovery. "'This is Serious,' said Pooh. 'I must have an Escape.'"[36] An assessment of the problem, and an immediate decision to address it, a call to action: Pooh lines up his pots of honey, ten in all, along a branch of the tree above his house, where he began to wait out the storm with a full supply of provisions. When those are all empty Pooh sees Piglet's bottle floating past. Thinking it may be more honey (and thus allowing him to extend his plan), he retrieves the bottle. Discovering that it contains not honey, but rather a letter, Pooh (not able, himself, to read) determines that he needs to go find some help decoding the letter's message. "Only I can't swim. Bother!" says Pooh.[37] Fortunately, "Then he had an idea," says the narrator.[38] The idea is to use one of his larger honey pots as a flotation device. He names the pot, "The Floating Bear," and drifts off to find someone, not who can save him from the flood (he already has done that for himself) but who can decode the note for him, his freshest challenge.

It is only after he does find Christopher Robin and learns that the note indicates that Piglet needs help, that Pooh identifies saving Piglet as the next major goal and (seeing that his honey pot, The Floating Bear, is too small for both him and Christopher Robin) moves on to the next phase of problem-solving. In fact, this realization begins with (or perhaps is facilitated by) Pooh's own honest assessment of his first creation: "it isn't just an ordinary sort of boat. Sometimes it's a Boat, and sometimes it's more of an Accident. It all depends."[39] So, when Christopher Robin notes that "it's too small for two of us," Pooh is comfortable observing the further need, "Three of us with Piglet."[40] Then, rather than jumping in with his own solution, the boy asks, as if trusting the bear's handle on the situation, "Oh, Pooh Bear, what shall we do?"[41] Pooh, after no small array of narrative fanfare, calmly answers, "We might go in your umbrella."[42]

And indeed, upside down, Christopher Robin's open umbrella serves perfectly as a vessel for the boy and the bear to float off to rescue Piglet, leaving ample room for the latter to join them when they arrive at his flooded house. The umbrella is such a great suggestion as a boat that Christopher Robin christens it, *The Brain of Pooh*. Open, roomy, applied inventively, situationally, humanely, and effectively, it seems the perfect description of both the umbrella and the brain.

To further sharpen by contrast Pooh's "growth mindset," let's go back through the stories (and leap ahead to one not yet considered) to take a look at a few characters whose minds are variously "fixed." Rabbit, for example. When Pooh gets stuck in his doorway after eating too much honey during his visit, Rabbit doesn't see or respond to that problem so much as an opportunity to learn more about having a roommate, for example, or even about the usefulness (moving forward) of an interior torso as a clothing rack. He is primarily interested in returning to his regular routines as quickly and easily as possible. Even his plan to use Pooh's legs for hanging clothing is a way of adapting to (what he hopes to be) a temporary situation, not a way of expanding his knowledge of interior design. Throughout the stories, Rabbit works as an expert. He is an expert (or at least he considers himself so) at gardening, which radiates out to his pronouncements about other such matters as weather conditions, planting and weeding techniques, and the timing of a perfect harvest. However, in none of those contexts is Rabbit ever portrayed as being uncertain enough to learn from anyone else (or even from his own experiences). He considers failures to be not lessons to inform future modifications but rather embarrassing marks on his skills, knowledge, and by extension his character.

An equally fixed character, but who shows relatively little sense of superiority or the embarrassment that comes from having that superiority questioned is Piglet. In their hunt for Woozles, Pooh and Piglet are equally humbled by the mystery, but in contrast to Pooh who sees the mystery as a curiosity to be explored further, Piglet sees it rather quickly as a threat to be escaped, a risk to be avoided, a challenge whose consequences promise not growth but risk, and ultimately, almost certainly, harm. Later, when Piglet is responding to the rising floodwaters, even his action is passive, sending out calls for help and then waiting for help to arrive. At no point does he either make efforts to survive in place (as is Pooh's first instinct) or take action to escape the increasing peril (as, again, does Pooh in recognizing that he can use his empty honey pot as a boat). Piglet operates from a narrow and limited definition of his own skills and potential, and at no time, even when any of those skills seems to apply to his situation, does he push himself to increase the range of those skills, or even adapt a simple skill to an unfamiliar problem.

Eeyore is essentially a cliché for learned helplessness. His pessimism is so complete and resolved that even when he experiences success through the help of a friend he questions its validity. The closest he comes to mental adaptability is in the chapter titled, "Eeyore Has a Birthday." It is in this chapter where Eeyore receives a balloon from Pooh, only by the time he receives it, Pooh has fallen on the balloon and popped it. Once Eeyore discovers that the balloon is red ("My favorite color") and "about as big as [Pooh]," which Eeyore acknowledges as, "My favorite size," the donkey is truly grateful for the gift, no matter its roughened condition.[43] I wouldn't argue that in those moments or the one where he receives his missing tail, Eeyore is ungrateful in spite of the circumstances that may otherwise have preoccupied Rabbit or Owl. But it is not Eeyore who finds his tail, and not Eeyore who endures the struggle that Pooh manages as he strives to deliver Eeyore's present. Eeyore's role, though open-minded and somewhat adaptable in adjusting his expectations, still is passive, with no apparent growth to come as a result of being given a popped balloon rather than one filled with air. He simply accepts what he has come to expect that he deserves, which isn't very much at all.

Owl's fixedness is caused by his traditional source of knowledge. His family history, with its tales and fables, informs his own sense of expertise as well as the stories he tells the others to justify that sense. He is, by the iconic power of his identity as an owl, wise. Milne, then, makes Owl's wisdom amusing to his readers by rendering it a mere pretentious entitlement, harmlessly pompous, verbose, and silly. As a result, he also makes Owl utterly uninterested in acknowledging mental gaps or seizing opportunities to learn more. Even when his spelling comically departs from the standard forms, his absurd word orientations stand for him not as signs of a need for improvement, but of his mental complexity and superiority. For basic spelling duties, the group would call upon Christopher Robin. Owl's thoughts, as Pooh implies, are far too deeply involved in matters of knowing "anything about anything," to be bothered with how to spell "buttered toast."[44]

In fact, more often than not, Owl is portrayed as thinking that he must dumb down his commentary, not expand it beyond his own range of intelligence. Case in point, his announcement to Christopher Robin, in chapter 9, that, "The atmospheric conditions have been very unfavorable lately," prompts the boy's request for him to clarify. Owl's reply, "It has been raining," elicits Christopher Robin's simple, "Yes . . . It has."[45] The boy's tone reinforces the obvious and simple nature of Owl's real meaning, a meaning that he first attempted to inflate with lofty, scientific rhetoric. Thus, saying that, "it has been raining," isn't really Owl's dumbing down his initial statement, but rather his stating an obvious point as it needed originally to be stated. Owl's first version is a stuffy translation, carrying not greater intelligence, but rather the pretense of greater intelligence. This pretense illustrates Owl's priority of sounding smart over his interest in actually becoming smarter. After all, he is Owl, *an* owl. Being smart is a characteristic, a defining, iconic trait, not a continuum.

To find a moving target, a reader has to go into a story that appears in the next collection, (*The House at Pooh Corner*) to the introduction of a character named Tigger. Arriving with such dynamism, bouncing and vocalizing all along the way, Tigger has the potential for a truly growth-oriented character. However, he is too focused on identifying himself and celebrating his defining, superlative characteristics to allow time and space for those traits to reveal weaknesses, and as a consequence of observant, strategic remediation, to grow. Tigger either solidly likes something, or he dislikes it. Everything exists in binary extremes. In his gregarious ebullience, Tigger seems too confident in himself to allow room for the vulnerability that carves out room between those extremes for patience, observation, and learning. For example, as he explores all of the things he is presented for eating, determined at first that he likes each thing he encounters, Tigger never tries something new as if liking it is *optional* or developmental. He only tries things that he announces that he already approves of, and then after tasting it declares, "Tiggers don't like" whatever it is he has just tried.

Even as Tigger explores his world, he lives between those two extremes: like/dislike, yes/know, bounce/ "un-bounce." In some respects, he is the opposite of Owl or Rabbit, whose preferences are so fixed that they fail to explore any new experiences, the opposite of Piglet or Eeyore who respectively are too afraid or too pessimistic to consider options beyond their current lot. Yet even as Tigger explores, he does so not to learn, nor to expand his options, but rather to confirm options, or as is more often the case, to cross them off.

Finally, as I have already mentioned, in spite of how supportive and encouraging he typically seems to be, Christopher Robin exhibits some of the most glaring examples of a "fixed mindset," especially with his unqualified and absolutist praise of Pooh's brilliance, but also with his often condescending role as the child whose imagination is bringing them all to life. The times when Christopher Robin appears most often is when his help is needed, either as a translator of language or provider of advice or comfort during particularly trying adventures. Even his warm, caring, "Silly old Bear," accepts Pooh's innocent shortcomings to the exclusion of the potentially valid ideas that may be percolating in the very moments that Christopher is patronizing as "silly." In that respect, and somewhat ironically, it is precisely when Christopher Robin's commentary is limiting Pooh's intellectual potential that the bear's intelligence stands out most clearly. These moments seem (as with The Brain of Pooh) to surprise the boy as much as they ever meet his expectations, and in either case the two hardly ever meet as equals, with room available for the questions of each.

One such rare time of balance is at the very end of the second collection, in the chapter titled, "In Which Christopher Robin and Pooh Come to an Enchanted Place, and We Leave Them There." The chapter begins, "Christopher Robin was going away."[46] It centers around his and Pooh's last conversation before the boy leaves for school. A literal reading of the transition would have Christopher Robin going away to boarding school, but the narrative more substantively addresses the transition from innocence to the period of life when any school learning begins to change a child into an educated human being. Christopher Robin initiates the conversation with Pooh about that transition by describing his love for doing "nothing." As he begins to detail how much nothing he has done so far in life there in an area of the woods called, "Galleons Lap," Christopher Robin tells Pooh about the numerous imaginary games, characters, and stories he has enjoyed while playing there. He teaches Pooh about imagination, even as (in the narrative's reality) Pooh, himself, is also a part of that imaginary world. However, in that conversation, as the boy faces the impending time for leaving that world, Pooh poses his own questions to Christopher Robin. It is a reciprocated sharing of questions about the unknown, with both characters offering questions and listening to responses. The boy's greatest concern is whether Pooh will still come to this, their favorite spot, once Christopher Robin has left for school. Pooh assures him that he will, and Christopher Robin assures Pooh that he (the boy) will be there with him. Of course, the boy will not physically be there, but he is promising Pooh that he will be there through his memory of those times. This could become a one-sided moment, one in which Christopher Robin tells his toys (or maybe his quickly fleeting childhood self) that he will always remember the beauty and magic of that childhood. But Milne doesn't let the conversation stop with just the boy's side.

In their post-card famous and often-portrayed interchange, Christopher Robin begins, "Pooh, promise me you won't forget about me, ever. Not even when I'm a hundred." Pooh's initial response is consistent with every growth-oriented inclination of his I have been reflecting on throughout this chapter: "Pooh thought for a little." Then he asks Christopher Robin a question: "How old shall *I* be then?"[47]

Two characters, contemplating the unknown as equals.

When Christopher Robin answers, "'Ninety-nine,' Pooh nodded, 'I promise,' he said."[48] It is a reasoned response.

Following this interchange, the next and final two things Pooh says to Christopher Robin take the form of questions. At first glance, they seem like suggestions (coming full circle) that Pooh is not particularly intelligent. Christopher Robin is trying to be more specific with Pooh about the irreversibility of the changes he is approaching:

"Pooh, *whatever* happens, you *will* understand, won't you?"
  "Understand what?"
  "Oh, nothing." He laughed and jumped to his feet. "Come on!"
  "Where?" said Pooh.[49]

Reading this final interchange with the presumption that Pooh is not dense but rather curious, one is ushered out of these stories and into Christopher Robin's formal education with a reminder of the simple, natural power of inquisitive open-mindedness—or rather, growth mindset. What is there to understand, and where is there to go? While Christopher Robin's upcoming tasks may be driven more by the acquisition of facts, the passing of tests, the moving along through grades, and the earning of degrees, Milne suggests that from Pooh he is learning a different approach to education, one that may help him navigate the years ahead in such a way so as never to stop asking questions, never to stop expanding his understanding or striking out in new directions, and never to forget his old friend, even when he's a hundred.

A. A. Milne almost certainly did not write *Winnie-the-Pooh* and *House at Pooh Corner* to make an explicit educational statement. However, what he illustrates through his toy characters' encountering of problems and his boy character's leaving for school and adulthood is the power of observation over judgment, thought over identity, questions over answers, risk over fear, action over surrender, and patience over the comfort of immediate gratification. Any student, whether human or stuffed bear, who is willing to ask, as does Pooh as his story comes to a close, what there is to understand and where there is to go, and wait attentively for the answers, will both extend the popular contemporary ideas about growth in education, and honor the educational legacy of Winnie-the-Pooh.

NOTES

1. A. A. Milne, *The World of Pooh: The Complete Winnie-the-Pooh and the House at Pooh Corner* (New York: E. P. Dutton & Company, Inc., 1957), 9.
2. Carole Dweck, *Mindset: The New Psychology of Success* (New York: Ballantine Books, 2006).
3. Angela Duckworth, *Grit: The Power of Passion and Perseverance* (New York: Charles Scribner's Sons, 2016).
4. Anders Ericsson, *Peak: Secrets from the New Science of Expertise* (New York: Mariner Books, 2017).
5. Carole Dweck, *Mindset: The New Psychology of Success* (New York: Ballantine Books, 2006).
6. Ibid.
7. Angela Duckworth, *Grit: The Power of Passion and Perseverance* (New York: Charles Scribner's Sons, 2016).
8. Ibid.
9. Anders Ericsson, *Peak: Secrets from the New Science of Expertise* (New York: Mariner Books, 2017).
10. Ibid.
11. A. A. Milne, *The World of Pooh: The Complete Winnie-the-Pooh and The House at Pooh Corner* (New York: E. P. Dutton & Company, Inc., 1957), 9.
12. Ibid., 9–10.
13. Ibid., 10.
14. Ibid.
15. Ibid., 13.
16. Ibid.
17. Ibid., 16–17.
18. Ibid.

19. Ibid., 18–19.
20. Ibid., 20–21.
21. Ibid., 21.
22. Ibid., 22.
23. Ibid., 32.
24. Ibid.
25. Ibid.
26. Ibid., 35.
27. Ibid., 42.
28. Ibid., 44.
29. Ibid., 51.
30. Ibid.
31. Ibid., 53.
32. Ibid., 54.
33. Ibid., 55.
34. Ibid., 125.
35. Ibid.
36. Ibid., 126.
37. Ibid., 127.
38. Ibid.
39. Ibid., 132.
40. Ibid., 133.
41. Ibid.
42. Ibid.
43. Ibid., 83.
44. Ibid., 50.
45. Ibid., 130.
46. Ibid., 298.
47. Ibid., 313.
48. Ibid.
49. Ibid.

Chapter 6

Always Winter, But Never Christmas

Narnia and High Stakes Testing

INTRODUCTION

In the very opening of C. S. Lewis' *The Lion, the Witch, and the Wardrobe*, the reader meets a teacher, "an old Professor." It is to his house that Peter, Susan, Edmund, and Lucy retreat to escape the bombing of London during World War II. Right away, with the reference to the professor, there is a model of teaching, which should, in a book about images of teaching in British children's literature, dominate the portrayal of education offered in this novel. However, this eccentric professor serves only as a recurring counterpoint to the darker, more prominent educational image that guides the novel's plot and themes. Acting in direct and sharp contrast to the professor's wise and reasoned perspective is a force in Lewis' novel that all too accurately conjures the specter of modern-day high stakes testing. It is, consequently, that specter that I want to trace throughout the novel, and it is the ultimate resolution of that intimidating, destructive force (including an affirmation of the good professor's approach) that I believe speaks directly to the contemporary debate about educational "accountability."

Before getting to the novel, let me offer a few definitions of "high stakes testing" and "the accountability movement." Starting with the Soviet launch of Sputnik, and renewed by the publication of "A Nation at Risk," American public education was increasingly characterized as "eroded by a rising tide of mediocrity that threatens our very future as a Nation and a people."[1] According to the report, American students did not know what they needed to know, and implicitly even worse, they did not know as much as their student-counterparts in other countries. As a consequence, the report warned, our country was "at risk" of weakening as a world leader. The seventies were over. Only a few hippie-holdouts were still interested in such radical notions as critical thinking, personal growth, or self-expression. In the era of "A Nation at Risk," a new generation of scholars began publishing highly popular books lamenting a national loss of "cultural literacy"[2] and promising to deliver, *What Your Sixth* [or First, or Tenth, etc.] *Grader Needs to Know*, a series edited by Hirsch[3] and fueled by the research of Ravitch and Finn.[4] In the spirit of identifying and teaching (so to speak) the knowledge presumably required for effective living in America, politicians became more and more interested in pursuing assessment programs that held schools and teachers accountable for delivering what students had been found lacking. That movement reached a significant peak with President George W. Bush's program, "No Child Left Behind." Under the terms of NCLB, "Congress declared that by 2014, 100 percent of American children . . . would be 'proficient' in reading and math, as measured by new state standardized tests to be given every year in grades 3 through 8, and at least once in high school."[5]

The pressures on teachers to teach to the test were among the more innocent consequences of the policy. Many teachers, pressured to deliver student results or lose their jobs and have their school potentially closed, began doctoring their students' results. In less nefarious scenarios, states (who were given the rights to set their own standards of proficiency) set those standards so low as to be academically meaningless, even punitive in another way—students were being deceived by their successful test scores that they were actually achieving authentic academic progress.[6] Meanwhile, schoolwork that would nurture meaningful learning and growth was being displaced by prep sessions aimed at passing each next end-of-year or end-of-course test.

One afternoon years ago, during the very peak of the first panicking surge of NCLB, I was catching up with a former student who'd returned to campus for an alumni meeting. She was in her first year at a nearby elementary school. Already she was questioning her career choice after realizing that goals for making a difference in children's lives had been reduced to helping them pass certain specific tests. That afternoon, she stopped by my office to vent. "My principal told us last week that if he catches anybody teaching anything but writing and math for the rest of the school year, that person would be fired on the spot!" Yes, the word she used was, "catches." It was mid-March. That would be over two more months of instruction devoted only to performance on tests in two academic subject areas. No science, no storytime, no art, no geography, and certainly no free time simply to think or imagine, or worse yet, to play—just math and writing. As a prize for their obedience, the teachers would be rewarded with the opportunity to keep their jobs and to stay out of trouble. Here is where we make the leap to *The Lion, the Witch, and the Wardrobe*.

THE READING

As I mentioned earlier, the novel begins when the children are removed from the city to the country house of a professor. That identification alone is sufficient to consider the house as a metaphor for school. They are, in fact, hiding out in the country away from the trouble happening a relatively short distance away in the city which is regularly being bombed by a ruthless aggressor attempting by force and murder to convert the entire world into their ideal image. One morning when the rain outside has made real-world discovery impossible and indoor routines boring, Peter, the eldest, suggests that they explore the house, "and that was how the adventures began."[7]

The portal to even grander adventures, and the title image of the book, is a wardrobe standing by itself in an otherwise empty room, which all of the children but Lucy, the youngest, decide to pass by. Lucy, however, "stayed behind because she thought it would be worth while trying the door of the wardrobe, even though she felt almost sure that it would be locked. To her surprise it opened quite easily."[8] After all, sometimes all it takes to learn something new is to overcome a bit of self-doubt, and try. The door to the wardrobe reveals first a line of coats and then a cold, crunchy layer of snow, and within a few steps, a distant lamp post in a land called Narnia. Within moments of entering Narnia, Lucy makes a friend, even though it is a character whose assignment is to betray her. Mr. Tumnus is a faun, and his original intent is to report Lucy to the White Witch as a "daughter of Eve." He quickly feels ashamed, abandons that intention, and becomes Lucy's ally. This is the effect of learning with integrity. Lucy has entered an unfamiliar world, one which treats her cautiously, even hostilely, at first, but one which her open curiosity wins over. One could make the case that these negotiations are how learning works when the people (human or faun) involved allow interactions to displace prescriptions and assignments.

However, once she returns to the country house, back through the wardrobe and into the room where she left, Lucy's learning is assessed against a more standard set of criteria. Simply put, Lucy's siblings don't believe her. What she reports doesn't make sense to their accepted definition and measure of reality. She is teased about her story, and eventually she stops trying to be believed. However, on the next rainy day, when she returns to Narnia through the wardrobe, her brother Edmund sees her and—not driven by curiosity, but rather by the desire to follow her lead and worse, "because he wanted to go on teasing her about her imaginary country"—goes in behind her.[9] As students go, Edmund is no Lucy. Consequently, with his cynical, even cruel frame of mind, Edmund's initial experiences in Narnia attract a very different kind of teacher.

He does not befriend, much less convert, a gentle character such as Mr. Tumnus, but rather is recruited by the leader of all things autocratic, insecure, and punitive in Narnia, the White Witch. The White Witch bribes Edmund's allegiance with the promise of power, and of treats—the obsessively tempting yet ever unsatisfying Turkish Delight. When he returns again with his younger sister to the house, Edmund does so as a spy. Because it furthers the cause he has been lured into, Edmund betrays Lucy and fuels his older siblings' doubts, claiming that the two of them had only been playing a game of make-believe.

Peter and Susan are pressed to believe either Lucy or Edmund. To settle this dilemma they turn to the Old Professor. He approaches their problem predictably by using one of the more traditional academic references: "Logic! . . . Why don't they teach logic in these schools?"[10] The professor then steps the children through the only three possibilities—that Lucy is lying, that she is crazy, or that she is telling the truth. Admitting that under normal circumstances, Lucy does not lie, and that through experience they know that she is not insane, they then question the possibility that she may be telling the truth, if only because what she claims seems so hard to believe. No time had passed during her disappearance, and she claimed to have visited a world separate from the one in which they were living. The professor is undaunted: "That is the very thing that makes her story so likely to be true."[11] He explains that it seems perfectly plausible that other worlds exist, and that they would almost by definition be governed by a time construct different from the world they occupy in the country house. "'Nothing is more probable,' said the Professor."[12]

In this narrative moment, then, there are several countervailing forces: That of the professor, with his open-minded logic, and that of "these schools" which the professor criticizes for not properly preparing students for applications of logic or encounters with mystery; that of Susan and Peter, with their honest efforts to make sense of an experience that does not follow the rules they have been taught to consider; that of Lucy who is a student of the house and (already) of Narnia, a student of her own experience; that of Edmund who is a student of promises aimed at manipulating his weakness; and that of the professor's most glaring counterpart, The White Witch, whose education aims not at opening her students' minds, but rather of manipulating their weaknesses into blind obedience, serving her own self-preservation while the "students," themselves, are turned to frigid stone. Let's start with the teachers, and then consider the students.

The first true teacher is not the professor, but rather the home itself where the children (especially, first, Lucy) explore, and the second likewise is Narnia, which Lucy finds while exploring the house. These two narrative settings are teachers in the purest sense because they offer "students" room to follow interests and respond to challenging experiences. They also serve instructional roles as they call (select?) students who are ready for their lessons.

The professor seems aware of this quality. First of all, he uniquely trusts the landscape both of his house but also of the alternate world. He seems to understand how that alternate world works, or at least that it necessarily must work mysteriously, and he accepts its mystery. Consequently, he is the expert teacher, not as a master of subject matter but rather as a guide through a learning process. In relation to the house and Narnia, the professor's work as a teacher is second hand, but he does seem clear about how to navigate these two learning settings. He calls upon his own education to help him, particularly with the application of logic and a belief in the possible (the word he uses is, "probable"). With that clarity, he helps the children learn from those settings by applying those tools.

The White Witch is a very different kind of teacher. She doesn't trust her environment, but rather controls it. She doesn't release her students to their own exploration and reflection, but rather controls them toward producing very specific outcomes. She manipulates them into providing information that she has determined to be important to her survival, and into expressing allegiance merely aimed at promoting her image and protecting her secrets. She rewards that allegiance, but with treats that only addict her followers into craving more and more of the reward and therefore doing more and more of her bidding. She punishes those who fail to do as they are told, and her punishment is cruel and absolute.

As regards the novel's students, the first ones to present themselves (as this writing has already implied) are the children, Peter, Susan, Lucy, and Edmund. Perhaps as the youngest, Lucy is the student most open to learning simply from her experience—motivated by curiosity, and trusting and observant in her environment. Peter and Susan, at least during the first chapters of the novel, are portrayed as open-minded learners, but they require a slightly more formal instructional program. They receive Lucy's experience second hand, so to speak, and then are left to evaluate its believability and worth. They do, at least, however, consider that as a question, instead of dismissing it as an absurdity, a "wrong answer." To help them sort through their learning, they consult the professor. It is he (understanding that these elder children need the more sophisticated tools of logic and memory) who presents them with the more Socratic series of questions that enable them to arrive at a reasonable conclusion about Lucy's account.

Edmund is a different student, still. He neither learns purely (innocently?) from experience nor openly from an objective application of logic. Edmund approaches his experience with an intervening agenda, and he reasons through his experiences with a bias toward certain interpretations and answers. Put another way, Edmund's resentment of his older siblings position him to respond to the promise of power without considering questioning whether that power has integrity. Put yet another way, he is the teacher's pet whose only validation (at least for the moment) comes from the teacher's praise. He learns quickly to seek that praise, instead of risking offending the teacher by thinking for himself. As students go, Edmund is one who unreflectively accepts the system's definitions of success, and who seeks his education by working the system. He performs to earn the system's rewards as compensation for being cheated (whether by gender, birth order, or general attitude) out of other, more elusive forms of power. In terms of this chapter's focus, Edmund cares a lot about his test scores.

To expand on these observations, however, requires entering Narnia and moving on into the main body of the narrative to examine how this "outcomes based" atmosphere has taken hold there, and how it affects the characters who have been living with it all along. After all, by the time Lucy finds her way there through the wardrobe, Narnia has been under the witch's spell for some indefinite period of time. It is a land frozen in fear. Even as Lucy moves through the wardrobe, the first sign that she is in Narnia is the presence of snow crunching underfoot. The whole of the land is covered with snow and ice. As the Faun, Mr. Tumnus explains, it is "Always winter and never Christmas."[13]

Mr. Tumnus is the first character from Narnia who enters the story, the first character Lucy meets on her first trip there. He is surprised to see her, mainly because one of his assignments from the White Witch is to find her (or someone like her, referred to as "a Son of Adam or a Daughter of Eve,"[14] which is a way of saying, a human). He appears shocked to have stumbled into one so suddenly, and to be challenged now to complete that assignment with one who seems so small and innocent, for whom he bears no ill will, and for whom his natural inclination is to be kind, not manipulative.

The back story on the Faun's assignment is that according to prophecy, Narnia will be transformed upon the arrival of two Daughters of Eve and two Sons of Adam. Tumnus explains to Lucy that he has been ordered to capture any Son of Adam or Daughter of Eve he may find and bring them to her. In that way, the White Witch can destroy those figures before they remove her from power. Mr. Tumnus isn't just being friendly as he encounters Lucy, he is trying (unsuccessfully, thanks to his own conscience) to kidnap her in order to deliver her to the White Witch as a prisoner. Yet he *does* have a conscience, and he soon confesses the White Witch's plot, his role in it, and the price of failure:

> She's sure to find out. And she'll have my tail cut off, and my horns sawn off, and my beard plucked out, and she'll wave her wand over my beautiful cloven hoofs and turn them into horrid solid hoofs like a wretched horse's. And if she is extra and specially angry she'll turn me into stone and I shall be only a statue of a Faun in her horrible house until the four thrones of Cair Paravel are filled.[15]

So, first of all, what a price! Second, how childlike is Mr. Tumnus' description of what the Witch will do, a veritable litany of punishments that border on panic and hysteria, carrying the melodrama, not of one guided by constructive, extrinsic motivation, but of one desperately frightened into irrational performance.

On the third trip through the wardrobe (once it has been determined that Lucy had, in fact, been telling the truth) all four of the children go into Narnia. By this time, Edmund has formed his alliance with the White Witch and Mr. Tumnus has been arrested. As the children begin to follow a robin, who seems to be leading them with some beneficial intention, Edmund begins casting doubt on both the robin and any efforts to find and help the Faun. "The Faun saved Lucy," Peter said. "He *said* he did," Edmund replies, "But how do we know?"[16] Edmund plants the seeds of doubt about the robin (whom Peter originally openly trusts), and under the guise of objectivity he questions the validity of what Lucy has led them to accept as true.

Meanwhile, the robin leads the children to their encounter with the residents of Narnia next to appear on the story, the Beavers. Unlike Tumnus, the Beavers are not so much servants of the Witch as they are anonymous citizens content for the time being only to avoid her wrath. They are, in that regard, the students who sit in the back of the room and keep their heads down, the students who turn in their assignments but avoid investing too much of their ego in the score listed at the top of each recently returned quiz. Edmund doubts the Beavers, as well. "How do we know you're a friend?" he asks.[17] Edmund needs to believe that the White Witch is good, and that his relationship with her is smart and right.

However, the real role that the Beaver's play in this system of high stakes testing I'm building a case for is as an informed, cautious general public, a public who knows what is going on, but feels no power to change what it sees as dangerous or corrupt. Consequently, they do what most members of the informed, powerless public do—they hide and wait for things to get better. Thus, on their first encounter, Mr. Beaver is careful, first about even being seen by the children, and then about sharing information with them. However, once the Beaver recognizes who the children are, he does his best to maneuver the group along to a place where they may speak safely. From their preliminary hiding place, the Beaver clarifies the children's identity more specifically, confirming that they are "Sons of Adam and Daughters of Eve." With that point established, he shows yet more background knowledge of the general circumstances in which he is living. There are spies among them: "There are trees that would betray us to *her*."[18]

He only begins to feel safe talking with them when they reach the Beavers' home. Safety, as well as an authenticity and a comfort, are represented by the meal that Mrs. Beaver prepares for them upon their arrival. This meal is no Turkish Delight, nothing here that merely tempts without nourishing. It includes boiled potatoes, fried trout, "a jug of creamy milk . . . and a great lump of deep yellow butter in the middle of the table from which everyone took as much as he wanted to go with his potatoes."[19] For dessert, Mrs. Beaver offers, "a great and gloriously sticky marmalade roll, steaming hot."[20] There is tea for all, and beer for Mr. Beaver. It is a bountiful, albeit simple, and very substantive feast. As such, it conveys the Beavers' appreciation for truth, trust, and wellness. Appropriately, this meal establishes the tone and serves as the prelude to a conversation about the role that the children will play in the novel's main plot piece, the return of Aslan and the removal of The White Witch, and thus the long-awaited move out of winter, through Christmas, and into spring. The return of Aslan, in other words, will mean a return to life. The Beavers know all about this prophecy, though they are powerless to make any of it happen, or so they believe.

There is power, however, even in the knowing. For in knowing, they know whom to trust, and with whom to communicate, and consequently, whom to empower. They are, in this respect, not just general citizens, but themselves aware and daring teachers.

By the time this conversation is happening, Edmund has gone missing. He is made immediately uncomfortable by what Mr. Beaver is saying about the White Witch, is tempted again by his thoughts of the Witch and her manipulative promises, and is determined to see her as the "good" force in this system, while defining any character who questions her as the one who should be doubted. Also by this time, Mr. Tumnus has been captured, turned to stone for betraying the very agenda that Edmund is trying to convince himself is right. Then, after hearing Mr. Beaver's account of a change already detected, signs that Aslan is on the move, Peter, Susan, and Lucy go out to stop the Witch, who will be "on the move" as soon as Edmund tells her that they are in Narnia. As these forces all go into motion, the narrative provides the perfect opportunity for meeting (or more completely examining) its two main characters, Aslan and The White Witch.

It is the latter to whom Edmund first reports, so it is she whose true character will be considered first. Even Edmund knew, "deep down inside him . . . that the White Witch was bad and cruel."[21] As he approached her house in the snowy night, he is described as being afraid of its appearance. "But it was too late to think of turning back now."[22] The house's courtyard is scattered with statues of once living creatures, now turned to stone, and a wolf guards the threshold. The wolf ushers him in to the witch, and she meets him not with her former welcome, but with rage that he has come alone, and even more rage at his story from the Beavers about Aslan's recent progress.

When he asks for more Turkish Delight, she orders him only dry bread, and when the woodland animals report to her that they have seen "Father

Christmas," she becomes further enraged. Snow begins to melt, flowers begin to push through the warming ground, and as all signs begin to reinforce the return of Aslan, the White Witch becomes more and more angry and violent. This is a multiple choice test, and the teacher is looking for but one answer. Any growing pressure from a countervailing truth will only insult and threaten her clearly waning authority. The agenda becomes less about promoting an effective strategy (and even less about debating relatively effective strategies) than about defending the status quo, protecting the established order, not just because it has been so long invested in, but also because it is an extension of the "teacher's" ego. All of these enterprises leave courtyards strewn with stony, frozen figures—teachers who have lost their passion for the classroom, students who have learned to equate learning with test scores, politicians (from school board members to state legislators) who care more about promoting "accountability" (when tough language earns them votes) than about educating principals to empower teachers to inspire students.

Consistently, it is an awareness and open acknowledgement of the flaws in traditional assessment systems that inspire periodic development of more situational, more personal, more authentic approaches to assessment. Portfolios, project-based instruction, peer assessment, journaling, service learning, even well-articulated rubrics are just a few examples of these more human and humane approaches. The signals in *The Lion, the Witch, and the Wardrobe* indicate that if The White Witch can be read as what I just called "traditional assessment," then Aslan is her humane alternative. One such signal is the associations between Aslan and the kinder, less corrupted characters—Tumnus, the Beavers, Lucy. Another is the effect of his return not only prophetically but experientially to Narnia, itself. Christmas arrives, represented by Father Christmas, portrayed in the novel as the cause for celebration and feasting. Life begins to return, as daffodils break through the melting snow. There is energy and movement, not stone and ice (themselves the very symbols of inertia and death). Beyond the effects created as Aslan approaches, however, are the actions and words issued once he is present, Aslan's instructional methodology, so to speak, his work as the educational counterpoint to the exacting, irrational, and punitive White Witch. What kind of teacher is Aslan?

In the first direct encounter the reader has with the great lion, Aslan has assumed the position often associated with classic teachers, in the center of a gathered crowd. The first emotional effect that Aslan causes, as is again the effect created by many great classic images of the teacher, is fear and awe. The narrative implies that Aslan is, "good and terrible at the same time," and the children "found they couldn't look at him and went all trembly."[23] But the first words out of Aslan's mouth are neither the saccharine lines of manipulation nor angry criticism, but rather words of recognition and welcome. He calls each of the three children (as well as Mr. and Mrs. Beaver) by name, and then misses the younger brother, Edmund. It is a roll call, of sorts, which comes before Aslan's laying out the learning task, both for saving Edmund and implicitly for saving Narnia.

He is as honest about the challenging nature of the task as he is about his personal, caring connection with them and his faith in what they can accomplish. Aslan's first official lesson is directed at Peter, "the first born," and therefore future, "High King over all the rest."[24] It is a substantive and experiential lesson with affirming and authentic assessment. Peter is placed into battle against a wolf. Peter's first instinct is to run. Then realizing what he is being called to do, and why the call is so significant, Peter finds the courage to fight, and the skills and tenacity to defeat the wolf. In recognition for his success, Aslan makes two significant gestures: he reminds Peter about the importance of cleaning his sword (pragmatic feedback); then he uses that cleaned sword for the purposes of delivering substantive, praise, dubbing the victor, "Sir Peter Wolf's-Bane."[25] The title is both extrinsic and relevant directly to his accomplishment, a celebration that is a worthy extension of the success.

The White Witch rules differently. When Aslan asks her to comment on Deep Magic, his intent is a challenge, a test of her true knowledge. Her reaction is to remind him of her sense of her punitive power: "You know that every traitor belongs to me as my lawful prey and that for every treachery I have a right to kill."[26] The Beaver, who is standing nearby, observes that the witch attempts to access power via the mere delivery of punishment, and claims her right to exercise that perversion of power merely via her title of Queen.

In the end, it is not only Deep Magic, but "a deeper magic from before the dawn of time"[27] and Aslan's knowledge of that deeper magic, that saves him from the Witch's destruction. That magic is activated, "when a willing victim who had committed no treachery was killed in a traitor's stead."[28] This is what happens when Aslan takes Edmund's place to receive the Witch's punishment. It is that willing sacrifice that inspires Edmund to fight more fiercely and gallantly than anyone in the final battle to defeat the Witch's army. Reading this plot segment with an eye to authentic assessment, once Edmund realizes that his actions are being rewarded with substantive, not superficial, appreciation and responsibility, not only does he choose those further actions over the pettier previous ones, but chooses as well the "teacher" who trusts his potential and takes risks to demonstrate that trust is saved, as well, tapping into a sense of right (a deeper magic) that far exceeds a "cut off" score on a standardized test.

Edmund doesn't just pass a test (though he does do that), he discovers a greater power within himself; he learns something previously out of reach about who he is and what he can do. By the time that learning is being put to action, Aslan no longer needs to mark it with a test score, or an "A." Everyone who remembers Edmund's performance in battle naturally acknowledges and admires his heroism: "We'd have been beaten if it hadn't been for him."[29] It is obviously no glamorous work! When the children find their brother, "he was covered with blood, his mouth was open, and his face was a nasty green color."[30] Lucy wants to help him, and pours a few drops of a life-saving elixir into his mouth, but Aslan guides her to the many others who also need help. She has to trust in the elixir and go to offer its help to those with whom and for whom Edmund had fought. It isn't just about saving her brother, Aslan indicates. "Must more people die for Edmund?" he asks.[31]

This moment offers Lucy her lesson in trust—trust in the magic, trust in her brother, and trust in herself to expand her influence beyond just that arena about which she cares the most selfishly. Predictably (by now) in Lucy's absence to go around caring for others, Edmund recovers. When she returns, he is looking, "better than she had seen him look . . . since his first term at that horrid school which was where he had begun to go wrong."[32] For his performance at "that horrid school," one can imagine he was abused in one way or another, perhaps Hook-like in the way he is turned into the resentful, deceitful child we meet early in the novel. He went wrong, one might imagine, having been treated wrongly, and as if he were "wrong." For his performance in battle, for channeling the deep forces of good and applying those forces selflessly and sacrificially, Edmund begins to transform those old, conditioned definitions of himself and is given new life. In fact, "he had become his real old self again and could look you in the face."[33] Only then (as was his elder brother earlier), after feeling and expressing the fullness of a legitimate transformation, is Edmund offered the symbolic recognition of his new status, and dubbed a knight.

In a public statement during the height of collective complaints that his "No Child Left Behind" program was forcing teachers to "teach to the test," President George W. Bush quipped, "If the test tests for what children need to know, then what's wrong with that?" It was the same concern about trendy applications of E. D. Hirsch's list of terms that every culturally literate American should know. No matter how much Hirsch attempted to clarify that the terms in his list reflected knowledge that people should accumulate through substantive school learning, not mere list-memorization, mere memorization was how many teachers were pressured to deliver "cultural literacy." The fact that the list, itself, comprised the last quarter of the book helped reinforce that approach. For many, that approach satisfied a deeply held belief that learning is a linear act of solving a problem, and that once a deficiency has been identified, the smartest and most effective way to remediate that deficiency is to attack it directly, the way one might fix a leaky faucet or replace a spark plug.

Much assessment, especially what I have been referring to here as high stakes assessment, operates that way, because much of it is motivated (starting with "A Nation at Risk") by an urgency to fix something that is broken. What Lewis' novel portrays is "a deeper magic," one that in instructional terms often looks inefficient—like small group discussion, peer review, journaling, writing across the curriculum, portfolio development, and holistic assessment. These (and other similar) approaches attempt to transform class-room instruction into meaningful experience. Consequently, they are often far more interested in processes and motives than in outcomes and answers. In the world of program assessment, one advantage to outcomes and answers, however, is that they sit still, they appear in score boxes, and may be reported in lists. They promise something comforting: certainty. That's how ice and stone work, too. They are static and therefore highly predictable, measurable, and controllable. The problem is, they are also utterly lacking in life.

But as winter turns to spring, ice begins to thaw, things get muddy, plants emerge where seeds may have been dropped the season before without any-one's knowing, seedlings sprout where squirrels have buried and forgotten acorns. Streams trickle from melting snow, and sometimes that trickle swells rivers into areas unprepared for the floods. Spring is unpredictable, yet it is very real. It looks you in the face, and its rewards are natural. So it is with academic assessments. The most natural and rewarding ones operate through their connections with the nature of the learner. A roomful of statues is much more easy to control and measure than a roomful of third graders, but the noblest outcomes of education aren't achieved by treating third graders like statues, and the nature of third graders doesn't cooperate particularly well with being treated as if that is the goal.

Aslan doesn't control Edmund through bribes and punishments. He enables Edmund to recover the means for controlling himself. This recovery begins as a gift to the boy greater than any that might be brought by Father Christmas, and yet marks only the beginning of a life of continued, even heroic growth. With more Christian allegory in mind than a study of students finally freed from an unrelenting battery of multiple choice tests, the spirit of C. S. Lewis might shake his head at this reading of Narnia. And yet, to experience the false promises and Turkish Delight at work in cut-off scores and measures of Adequate Yearly Progress is to see how high stakes testing creates the very same kind of eternal winter in American education.

NOTES

1. *A Nation at Risk: The Imperative for Educational Reform* (Washington, DC: U.S. Government Printing Office, April 1983).

2. E. D. Hirsch, *Cultural Literacy: What Every American Needs to Know* (New York: Vintage Books, 1988).

3. E. D. Hirsch, ed., *What Your 6th Grader Needs to Know* (New York: Doubleday, 1993).

4. Diane Ravitch and Chester Finn, *What Do Our 17-Year Olds Know?: A Report on the First National Assessment of History and Literature* (New York: HarperCollins, 1989).

5. Dana Goldstein, *The Teacher Wars: A History of America's Most Embattled Profession* (New York: Anchor Books, 2014), 185.

6. Ibid.

7. C. S. Lewis, *The Lion, the Witch, and the Wardrobe* (New York: Harper Trophy, 1994), 6.

8. Ibid.

9. Ibid., 27.

10. Ibid., 48.

11. Ibid., 49.

12. Ibid., 50.

13. Ibid., 19.

14. Ibid., 20.

15. Ibid., 19–20.

16. Ibid., 62.

17. Ibid., 67.

18. Ibid.

19. Ibid., 74.

20. Ibid.

21. Ibid., 89.

22. Ibid., 92.

23. Ibid., 126.

24. Ibid., 130.

25. Ibid., 133.

26. Ibid., 142.

27. Ibid., 156.

28. Ibid., 163.

29. Ibid., 178.

30. Ibid., 179.

31. Ibid.

32. Ibid., 180.

33. Ibid.

Chapter 7

How Bilbo Learns

Environmental Inquiry and Reflective Practice in The Hobbit

INTRODUCTION

Throughout the 1980s and into the 1990s, University of Chicago English and Education Professor, George Hillocks, Jr., investigated three modes of instruction: Presentational, Naturalistic, and a mode he called, "Environmental Inquiry." Presentational mode is essentially lecture, and naturalistic modes are represented by the various examples of learning so prevalent in the 1980s such as free writing, journaling, and other student-centered, largely unstructured, and unguided activities. Environmental Inquiry was unique because of its combination of student autonomy and carefully prepared task structures.[1] His meta-analysis of studies of composition instruction, as well as his own research on writing students (across grade levels from middle and high school to community college) show holistic scores of quality continuing to rise on papers produced in environmental classes even in delayed posttests.[2] In other words, unlike its pedagogical counterparts used with control groups, under the conditions of Environmental Inquiry (a mode Hillocks came to refer to as "reflective practice")[3] writing skills continued to improve even after the instruction was complete, indicating that a part of what students learned was not just how to write the paper in question, but rather how to build writing skills that they themselves could reflect on and apply more powerfully with further practice.

Of course, the inquiry didn't start with Hillocks. It echoes at least from Dewey, forms the basis of the Montessori method, and extends into more contemporary models of "project-based learning," case study pedagogy, and scientific experimentation. While the teacher's role is to create an intentional and engaging environment, it's the environment itself that is the true teacher once an inquiry-based classroom is underway. The teacher's most important task isn't to control the students or the information, but rather to front-load his or her work into preparing the materials and space for student experience.[4] For Montessori, this means preparing explicitly designed materials so that a child who is ready to work with that material (Montessori teachers actually refer to the material as a "work") will not need further guidance from anything except the material and his or her own physical (and therefore cognitive) interactions with it.[5] To extend that model into *The Hobbit*, Tolkien, along with his pedagogical proxy, Gandalf, are the classroom teachers, but the environment which facilitates Bilbo's inquiry, his project station, his Montessori classroom full of works, is the very environment of Middle Earth. The result in all the above instances is a highly reflective and increasingly informed enterprise of trial and error, leading (as with Hillocks' middle schoolers) to an education that continually expands.

THE READING

"In a hole in the ground there lived a hobbit."[6] We've already seen at least one character whose education begins in a hole, but the Mole from Grahamme's novel already is tired of his subterranean life and launches his own journey out into the first challenges of his education. Not so for the hobbit. "It was a hobbit hole," the narrator explains, "and that means comfort."[7] Bilbo revels in his home's "comfort," and is completely devoted to the hobbit's calm, local life devoid of adventure. However, two forces intervene in that peaceful life: a family connection with the Tooks, whose penchant for adventure is nearly scandalous in contrast to the sedate Bagginses; and a wizard named Gandalf. Bilbo is perfectly happy not to be living the life of his more rambunctious relatives, and on the evening when Gandalf shows up, Bilbo is neither ready for nor interested in company, not from a wizard, and certainly not from the collection of dwarves who arrive shortly thereafter. Motivated more by a hobbit's inclination toward hospitality than any drive for adventure, Bilbo sufficiently feeds and entertains the wizard and dwarves, awaking the next morning to his quiet hobbit hole again thinking happily that all the excitement has passed. It is as if he has survived the in-class recitation activity without being called upon, and the bell has now rung as he returns home to another day of avoiding his assignment. However, for Bilbo such is not the case. Gandalf reappears to alert him to a note that the dwarves left before their much earlier departure. The note requests his presence, and informs him that he has only minutes before the appointed time. With Gandalf's urging, Bilbo leaves (as many reluctant learners do) without having sufficient time to fully prepare. The message seems to be that for some lessons there really is no conscious preparation, or perhaps that often preparation is a myth, a contrived sense of "getting ready" that simply puts a positive spin on procrastination. Or perhaps this detail is more to illustrate the difference between preparation and readiness.

In either case, Bilbo is launched on his journey, ready or not, and for the first few days and experiences he does little other than wish he were back in calm safety of his home. All signals are, however, that Bilbo is not only ready but perfect for the challenges that lay ahead. For starters, as he listens to the dwarves' songs, "something Tookish woke up inside him."[8] Then, as even the dwarves are questioning their appointed "burglar," Gandalf reassures them that he, himself, has placed the mark on Bilbo's door. "Let's have no more argument. I have chosen Mr. Baggins and that ought to be enough for all of you. . . . There's a lot more in him than you guess, and a deal more than he has any idea of himself."[9] In educational terms, I read this identification not so much as an acknowledgment of Bilbo's giftedness, but rather as Gandalf's faith in Bilbo's potential. If there is (and I think there is) an invitation to see Bilbo's Tookish ancestry as a special mark preparing him for this adventure, it can also mean that Tookishness is not the sole domain of the Baggins's, but rather a power that anyone may access for confidence and authority.

Bilbo's first two trials, however, are not particularly confident or powerful, and both end not with Bilbo's victory but with Gandalf coming to his rescue. When Bilbo is sent out to investigate a fire and any food it may afford, what he discovers is a pack of trolls roasting mutton. Being by trade a burglar and a pickpocket, Bilbo reached into the pocket of one of the trolls and stole its purse. This momentary achievement is where the success of his first initiative ends, as the troll notices the hobbit, which launches another phase of many typical first efforts—chaos, followed by novice and ultimately unsuccessful improvisation and adaptation. In this case, Bilbo stalls and distracts the trolls long enough for his companions to arrive, and when they are themselves unable to sort out the trolls even as group, Gandalf arrives with something many good teachers provide to students who've been struggling with a problem on their own long enough—relief. Gandalf distracts the trolls with magical deception until the sunrise turns them all to stone.

It would happen again with the next challenge. The travelers need their wizard to help them escape a treacherous jam in which goblins are chasing them deep into their warren of caves and tunnels. In the Vygotskian sense of scaffolding, the lessons for Bilbo begin with his being tapped as a worthy student, and then placed into situations that challenge his old ways, old knowledge, and old sense of himself. As he begins to experience challenges that are at the front end (so to speak) of his zone of proximal development, he needs a higher level of teacher support, a.k.a., being bailed out by Gandalf. Hillocks might explain this scene as an opportunity provided by a teacher knowledgeable enough about learning, as well as about the educational environment, to trust the student's autonomy, yet know how to tend to the boundaries that guide effort. Montessori, likewise, would realize that the main job of teaching in these early moments is to trust that whenever the task becomes unworkable the student will naturally stop engaging, stop learning, and seek help.

In the goblins' caves, this second rescue projects Bilbo forward (not only figuratively but literally) more deeply into the caves, alone, until he reaches the site of his first truly independent learning moment. By this time, Bilbo has found a curious object on the floor of the cave, a ring. At the bottom of the cave, he finds a body of water. On an island in that body of water lives a creature named Gollum. Gollum is described as having the potential to eat Bilbo, but is portrayed as being a bit more interested, temporarily at least, in enjoying Bilbo for conversation than as a meal. Consequently, the threat posed by Gollum is less urgent than the ones posed by the trolls or goblins, and the method of escaping Gollum relies more on strategy than force. In his encounter with Gollum, Bilbo is on his own, but he seems from the beginning to have more time and resources to manage the task.

The two skills he calls upon first are those that we know he brings with him. He already has been identified as a burglar, and so Bilbo has pocketed the ring. Second, he admits to being good at riddles, and so it is by an exchange of riddles that Bilbo outwits and therefore not only gets past, but also utilizes, even unwittingly exploits, Gollum. The riddles are, in fact, Gollum's idea. He proposes exchanging them as a distraction for his hunger. Bilbo agrees to the game, craftily asking Gollum to go first. They exchange riddles and solutions on equal terms, which offers the reader a chance to see yet one more aspect of Bilbo's intelligence, as well as an adaptability he is developing. Also, this test shows the first time in which Bilbo has the skills, himself, that he needs to overcome a problem. He will no longer need his teacher, Gandalf, at least not in this case, to provide him with boundaries or support. Finally, he ends the riddle exchange and successfully escapes from Gollum by calling upon his newfound power contained within his pocket, the ring.

Bilbo's final riddle (or rather, question) is simply, "What have I got in my pocket?"[10] This question comes at a point in the riddle exchange when it has become clear that Bilbo is an equal match to Gollum, likely even Gollum's superior and victor. Becoming desperate, Gollum asks for "one more question,"[11] perhaps a verbal mistake on Gollum's part, not asking for a riddle, and so opening up the game's rules to include Bilbo's different and ultimately unanswerable contribution. However, Bilbo's question was far more reactionary than any intentional strategy. Scrambling in his mind for a good riddle, his hand touches the ring in his pocket, and he blurts out his final question. It is a question that at first upsets Gollum: "Not fair! Not fair!"[12] But as I have just noted, Bilbo is completely fair, responding to Gollum's request for a "question," not a "riddle." The next level of panic from the underground creature is to guess wrongly and repeatedly through several attempts. Then, returning to his lair in an apparent attempt to stall on delivering his promise to help Bilbo escape the cave, Gollum notices that his "birthday present" (the ring) is missing, soon suspecting that Bilbo had stolen it. This realization launches a chase, instead of Gollum's promised guidance from the cave, and the chase prompts Bilbo to implement his final strategic maneuver of this confrontation, a maneuver that will become central to overcoming his future challenges. He reaches into his pocket, slips the ring onto his finger, and (under its power) disappears. Not only does this disappearance immediately relieve him from one problem (being attacked by Gollum), but it also solves the original problem of his escape as now he can simply follow Gollum up from the cave as the little creature goes off, ironically, in search of the now invisible Bilbo.

These tactics of the hobbits are noteworthy not only for their effectiveness and their direct application of Bilbo's knowledge and skills and disposition, but also for their illustration of the little hobbit's willingness to practice these traits as an improvisation, in their developing and incomplete forms. As a learner, Bilbo Baggins takes leaps of faith, enjoys outcomes he may not have achieved if he'd waited until he felt ready to leap at all, and learns things as a result that will be useful later in ways he may not have anticipated through a more proactive "education." The most important outcome of this educational success may well have been not his escape from Gollum, but rather the confidence in himself that comes from accomplishing that escape. It is an outcome that no teacher, other than sheer experience, has to provide or praise.

Consequently, he is ready a bit farther along the journey to help Thorin (the more traditionally authoritative dwarf) when the group comes to river whose crossing options are not immediately obvious. Bilbo sees a boat on the far side and proposes that they pull it to them with a rope. Thorin responds skeptically, "The boat is sure to be tied up, even if we could hook it, which I doubt."[13] At this point, Bilbo's openness kicks in. He doesn't accept that the boat is tied and encourages them to try to dislodge it, anyway. Bilbo's persistence and coaching result in the group's eventually hooking the boat, pulling it loose even though it did turn out to be tied up, loosening the occasionally snagged rope, and in time and with steady effort and adaptation, implementing the plan and crossing the stream.

If the escape from Gollum is a one-two punch, with the first punch featuring the use of intelligence and wit as riddler, and the second the use of magic as ring bearer; then the stream crossing described above is the first part of another one-two punch with an audience, the second part occurring a bit later as the travelers are captured by a group of giant spiders. In that captivity, with all hope seeming to be lost and no Gandalf in sight, Bilbo decides that he has to let his fellow travelers know about the ring. The dwarves only barely grasp the nature of what Bilbo is relating. Such a power, like any overwhelmingly new knowledge, is beyond their capacity to comprehend. Yet, recognizing the time to act, Bilbo slips on the ring and disappears. His stealthy work in battling the spiders slowly makes sense to the dwarves, and together they defeat the monsters. Here, Bilbo receives his first recognition from his fellow travelers, and their appreciation helps him see and believe in his success more clearly, more personally, and more confidently.

That feeling would be helpful for their very next challenge as, before finding their way out of the forest, barely a conversation into the next day, as exhausted and hungry they are debating the best path to use, they are taken prisoner by elves. It is again Bilbo who uses a combination of his ring's power and his own observation and ingenuity to create a plan for their escape, hidden away in barrels emptied and destined for floating downstream to market. This solution does not occur to Bilbo as a flash of brilliance, and once he begins to put the plan together in his mind he still isn't sure it will work. Even once he decides to implement the plan, the execution is not simple. There are steps, each one risky. First, Bilbo has to use the ring in order to disappear and steal the guard's keys. Then, he must go around and unlock all of the doors to where his friends are being held captive. Even after this noisy and chaotic step is complete, before loading up the dwarves into the respective barrels, Bilbo realizes that the hardest part of his plan may well be convincing his comrades to play along. His concerns are justified as the dwarves do, in fact, resist his plan as both dangerous and (even if successful) uncomfortable.

This is a phase of Bilbo's education when he not only questions his knowledge (as he has done earlier) but rather has that knowledge questioned by an external source. Consequently, he has to characterize that task to himself in a more complex way, a way that enables him to articulate it to others, and then his belief in its likely outcome. The dwarves' resistance prompts Bilbo to stand up for his own plan. Finding himself in a situation that may call for considering other options, he simply announces that unless they are willing to move forward with his plan, he will put them back into their prison cells, lock the doors again, and return the keys. It is in that sense Bilbo's escape plan or nothing. He is confident in what he has learned, and his confidence is what's needed to move the group forward: "In the end, of course, they had to do just what Bilbo suggested."[14]

I pause for a moment to note the progression—from blind grasper at what only accidentally became the ring of power, to nervous and improvisational exchanger of riddles, to hopeful and then intentional wearer of the ring, first for a fortuitous and then for a strategic outcome, and finally (for now) to intentional applications of both the ring and his wits, all accompanied by an increasingly complex knowledge of tasks and tools, and confidence in his plans to apply that knowledge to action. Bilbo is learning, and as he learns his efforts are producing increasingly significant outcomes. The group does use the barrels to escape. Their escape (along with the period of rest and recovery that follows it) allows them time and resources to become prepared for the ultimate purpose of their journey, an assault on Smaug and the recovery of the treasure the dragon is hoarding. So just like any series of powerful learning experiences, Bilbo's journey so far has only prepared him for even more challenging and consequential tests.

Either precisely aware of that fact, or attempting, in denial, to hope that his most difficult tasks are behind him, Bilbo rests in the grass as the group is floundering to locate the door to the dragon's lair, "'Perhaps the wizard will suddenly come back today,' he thought."[15] That would be really convenient, and yet the hobbit's thought isn't a harbinger of Gandalf's return, but rather the final expression of doubt just before his next epiphany. Even as Bilbo sits in something of a daze, a bird flies up and begins to crack open a snail's shell on the very place on the stone that marks the opening to the door. Then, remarkably and completely true to form, "Suddenly Bilbo understood."[16] He doesn't need Gandalf to help him after all, just a bit of quiet observation and a direct confrontation with his impulse to give up. Now, with the door unlocked and pushed open, what faces him is yet the next challenge: "It seemed as if darkness flowed out like a vapour from the hole in the mountain-side, and deep darkness in which nothing could be seen lay before their eyes, a yawning mouth leading in and down."[17] But Bilbo faces this next stage with an attitude different from the fear and hesitance, or even the blind guesswork of earlier days. He is energized by his now long-developed achievements and the cumulative knowledge they have provided, and he is buoyed by a new level of trust in himself.

With this jolt of confidence, Bilbo takes three journeys out on his own near the end of this saga. In the first, he not only confronts the dragon, but engages him in conversation. In the second, he wanders back into Smaug's lair and across his pile of treasure, where he finds the Arkenstone, the jewel of Thorin's family. In the third, he uses that Arkenstone as a bargaining chip with the Bard, a representative of a rival faction (a community destroyed by the rampaging Smaug, now looking for their own share of Smaug's treasure). I want to look at these journeys one at a time, to notice any patterns of Bilbo's continued growth.

As with his earlier conversation with Gollum, Bilbo's meeting with Smaug begins with uncertainty and a hopeful, yet fragmentary knowledge of how to proceed. At first, he operates exclusively as a burglar, moving quietly around the base of the hill where the dragon slept, lifting "a great two-handled cup" and fleeing when the beast seemed on the verge of waking.[18] After showing off the booty of this first raid, he offers to make a second visit, this time using his ring to become invisible, and this time going into the very chamber where the dragon slept. When Smaug awakens he taunts the hobbit unsuccessfully into coming closer so he can capture him. The two of them go far beyond the exchange of riddles, and into a substantive conversation full of Smaug's various rhetorical efforts to lure Bilbo in and Bilbo's return efforts to keep the dragon from finding out too much. "This of course is the way to talk to dragons," the narrator explains, "if you don't want to reveal your proper name (which is wise), and don't want to infuriate them by a flat refusal (which is also very wise)."[19]

This is the first passage that openly attributes wisdom to the little hobbit. It is a wisdom which denies the dragon Bilbo's actual name, and which in providing a variety of substitutes for that name, lists instead Bilbo's various achievements, all of which implicitly attribute that wisdom to those achievements. By the end of this conversation, Bilbo has located the dragon's one weak spot, a soft spot on his underbelly easily permeable to sword or arrow. Upon identifying this spot, Bilbo dashes away, but not before offering a parting joke that enrages the dragon that his prey has escaped. Bilbo's final thought as he leaves the dragon behind? "You aren't nearly through this adventure yet."[20]

It is while the now-enraged dragon is out venting his frustrations on the nearby countryside, that Bilbo returns to the treasure mound and finds the Arkenstone. He initiates this second journey with a self-conscious change of attitude: "I have been that way twice, when I knew there was a dragon at the other end, so I will risk a third visit when I am no longer sure."[21] To account for any confusion about trip-count, this is, indeed, Bilbo's third trip into the tunnel, though it is his second trip out among the final challenges that I am examining here. That being said, off the group goes again into the tunnel to the dragon's lair with the hobbit leading the way. The dwarves watch from the tunnel as Bilbo enters Smaug's chamber and climbs the mound of treasure in pursuit of the Arkenstone, "the Heart of the Mountain."[22] Bilbo is intrinsically gratified at the sight of it. "At last he looked down upon it, and he caught his breath. The great jewel shone before his feet of its own inner light."[23] With the jewel safely in his possession, Bilbo reflects, "Now I am a burglar indeed!"[24]

With the Arkenstone in his possession, the hobbit is now able to offer it to the Bard, leader of the opposition group, so that the stone may be exchanged for that group's rightful treasure, consequently brokering a peaceful resolution to their conflict with the dwarves. Bilbo, it would seem, isn't just a burglar but also a diplomat, capable not only of using courage to steal treasure from the dragon's lair, but then of knowing how to use that treasure for a larger, nobler purpose than the typical burglar's materialistic agenda. Bilbo sees the bigger picture in which the Arkenstone may be useful, and chooses that course of action because its outcome isn't just personal wealth or even family honor, but harmony between communities.

He also sees the more personal and immediate danger in using it as a bargaining chip. Just before he departs for the negotiation, he hears Thorin (whose family heirloom is the Arkenstone) going on and on about how valuable the piece is and how he will avenge any attempt to take it. Bilbo knows that he has committed that very act; not only that, but he already is planning albeit temporarily to give the stone away. Still, Bilbo knows that his imagined outcome is more important in the long run than Thorin's anger in the short run. While he admits to being worried about the possibility of failing, he quickly generates his resolve to trust in his plan and put it into action. "That night Bilbo made up his mind,"[25] illustrating yet another leap in confidence. Now, Bilbo (far beyond winging it) isn't just trusting his physical skill or wit; he believes in his intelligence and integrity, he believes in his strategy and the value of its ultimate payoff—the uniting of quarrelling factions and the re-establishment of fairness and peace.

Now, for the test of that belief—Bilbo's actual encounter with The Bard and the Elvinking, wherein he proposes his plan and delivers the stone. The first step of his plan is to buy himself some time to make his journey into the Bard's company. For that purpose, he arranges to take Bombur's shift on night watch. Then, instead of watching while Bombur sleeps, Bilbo goes off to meet with the Bard and the Elvinking. With Bombur asleep, there is no one to realize Bilbo has gone. Once he is near the Bard's camp, he slips on his ring and moves invisibly until he is close enough to reveal and identify himself to their elvin guards and calmly, confidently request a meeting with the Bard, himself. Once in the presence of the Bard, Bilbo speaks in the formal manner which the situation calls for, a manner which (it is appropriate to note) by this point not only does Bilbo know the importance of using, but also knows how to perform.

Then, Bilbo presents the potential threat of conflict to the Bard, as other groups of dwarves are on the move to help Thorin and engage in combat. With that threat established as a problem worth the Bard's attention, Bilbo's motives are clarified—"I am merely trying to avoid trouble for all concerned. Now I will make you an offer!!"[26] As he reveals the stone, the Elvinking, "stood up in amazement."[27] Their next caution is to note that Bilbo has stolen the Arkenstone, and so it may not rightfully be his to give. To that, he explains that he has been promised payment for his help to the dwarves from the beginning, and that he is, "willing to let [the stone] stand against all my claim."[28] In this gesture, Bilbo surrenders any other payment from the dwarves for service. Claiming the stone as his only payment, Bilbo is justified in using that stone as he wishes, including using it to help another party bargain for peace. Or, as Bilbo puts it, "I may be a burglar . . . but I am an honest one."[29]

For this successful negotiation, Bilbo receives two forms of authentic, contextualized praise. The first is from the Elvinking, who notes, "You are more worthy to wear the armour of elf-princes than many that have looked more comely in it."[30] He receives the second congratulations, as "an old man, wrapped in a dark cloak, rose from a tent door where he was sitting and came towards them. 'Well done! Mr. Baggins!'"[31] The old man in the dark cloak, it turns out, of course, is Gandalf, who has been monitoring the hobbit's growth and achievement from a distance. "There is always more about you than anyone expects!" the wizard says. As the fruits of his labor seem to be near at hand, and at least for now significantly appreciated, "for the first time for many a day Bilbo was really delighted."[32]

Placed as it is, after such a great plan's accomplishment but before its pay-off, the situation is analogous to asking on one's graduation day, "So, now that you have your degree, do you have a job?" That's the nature of formal education, after all, always being asked for the proof of its value, or in contemporary terms, "return on investment." From the perspective of reflective practice or environmental inquiry, the better question may be, "But, did it work?" Did Thorin accept the return of his family's stone in exchange for the gold owed to Bard and the Elvinking? In this case, Bilbo soon may answer clearly in the affirmative, though arriving at that point still has its challenges. Thorin, at first, is furious as one might imagine he would be at having his family's stone stolen, secretively held, then given away only so it may be offered back to him as leverage to insure a fairness. Yet, it is that fairness that he is persuaded to see—a fairness that is affirmed by Gandalf and honestly acknowledged by Bilbo himself, who admits to having taken the stone in the first place as his, "fourteenth share."[33] The Bard announces that he will keep the stone until receiving his share of the gold. Also, as unhappy as Thorin is with this deal, it is a deal which has been worked out according to Bilbo's original plan and resolved with integrity.

All that remains to be examined now is the final battle. The death of Smaug activates an army of Goblins and Wild Wolves to charge on the opposing army of Elves, men, and dwarves. It is Gandalf this time who makes the plan for defending against the Goblins. Bilbo finds a safe position among the Elves from which to observe. The battle raged all around him, but there was no "last desperate stand." In the end, The Eagles arrived, "in such a host as must have gathered from all the eyries of the North."[34] Bilbo is the first to see them, and as he calls out to cheer their arrival, he is knocked unconscious by a hurtling stone. By the time he regains consciousness they have defeated the Goblins, and the battle is over.

I read this moment in Bilbo's education as an opportunity, after all of his individual triumphs, to be simply present and a part of something greater than himself, which may be an important late-stage component of any good education. What remains now is (as I mention above) reconciliation, then a return to normal daily life, and finally the recording of his adventures for

Bilbo's own closure and clarification, and to provide an account of it for future "students" to read. And that is exactly how the novel ends.

First, immediately after the battle Bilbo is taken to Thorin who has been mortally wounded. The dwarf leader acknowledges his desire to "take back my words and deeds at the Gate."[35] In the moments before his death, Thorin tells Bilbo, "There is more in you of good than you know. . . . Some courage and some wisdom, blended in measure."[36] Thorin's words land well on Bilbo, who thinks after the dwarf's passing, "I'm glad that we parted in kindness."[37] He also expresses the kind of humility that is characteristic of the best of learning, admitting to himself, his blunders at negotiating with the stone and his failure to avoid the battle that cost Thorin his life. "I suppose you can hardly be blamed for that," Bilbo's self-directed thoughts continue, indicating that he is aware of having chosen the best path he could manage, and that in spite of its imperfection, he accepts its intention and its value.[38] With that parting thought, one may imagine Bilbo attempting similarly uncertain and imperfect gestures in future challenges, for further learning, so long as they are guided by attention, fairness, and honor.

The return home isn't easy, but it is shared with the company of Gandalf and (for a good part of the way) the shape-shifter, Beorn. As they return past the sites of earlier adventures, Bilbo reviews in his memory the events of those places, and by the time they reach Bilbo's own Hill, Gandalf remarks, "You are not the hobbit that you were.'"[39] Who would expect him to be? He has matriculated from an intensive and rigorous educational program, and education changes a person. It makes, and sometimes marks, him or her as new and different.

I enjoy thinking that, between the narrator's noting that his life was, "extraordinarily long"[40] and that his memoir writing was occurring "some years afterwards,"[41] between and even beyond that writing, Bilbo not only remained happy but also somewhat adventurous (albeit in terms acceptable for The Shire). The title of Bilbo's memoir implies yet another truth about education: "There and Back Again, a Hobbit's Holiday."[42] One could take it to mean that his education was confined to a time and a place—there and back, done—and that it was nothing more than a somewhat stressful vacation. However, the very existence of the memoir suggests that Bilbo continues to reflect on his experience, and the term holiday speaks to me less of vacation than of break from the norm and its drudgery. Bilbo has left the flow of his normal life for a time, and he has returned as a different person. These same words can describe a term in school (say, "fall semester") or even a level of education (middle school, high school, undergraduate study, there and back again, a holiday from my real life from which I return all new and "queer"). The journey to the Misty Mountain is Bilbo's holiday from being a hobbit, and as a result of going, he becomes, as Gandalf observes, "not the hobbit that you were." If you will remember, I make the same case a few chapters back regarding one's trip to Neverland.

Speaking of "back," it may be helpful to go back to the question implied in this chapter's title. How exactly does Bilbo learn?

First, he learns by nature, by disposition. He carries within him a force that distinguishes him from other hobbits, something Tookish, that makes him more prone to risk-taking and curiosity. I could say that all human beings carry that potential, and perhaps they do, but I don't think Tolkien's image of Bilbo conveys that point. Tolkien seems more clear that the internal powers that open the ways for learning are not distributed equally, nor to everyone. Some people like stability and stasis. Some people consider those who ask too many questions or who pursue adventures beyond the limits of their daily comforts to be strange, maybe even a little crazy. From a slightly different perspective, the message from Bilbo's Tookishness may be this: for any-one to learn, he or she must start from the posture of wanting more—more knowledge, more experience. That means that he or she must see the need for achieving more than characterizes his or her current state. So, even though he isn't acting on this trait in the beginning of his story, Bilbo does learn by wanting more, and that wanting comes from within him.

Bilbo, then learns from being identified externally as a candidate for the task. He is visited by Gandalf, who marks his door, and who already has sent out word to the dwarves. Not only is he identified as the candidate, but the skill he brings to the task is identified. He is a burglar. They don't just arrive on his doorstep because he will enjoy the journey. They need the very service he can provide if they are to sneak into Smaug's lair and steal the dragon's treasure.

Once Bilbo is identified, he is expected. Those who are calling him out to his lessons are uninterested in letting him decline their offer. After he real-izes they have not simply left, but are waiting for him to join them, Bilbo leaves without having a chance to feel ready. On several occasions, espe-cially in their early going, the whole group of travelers lose their provisions. On the morning of their departure, Bilbo even begins his journey without proper provisions. That's because yet another answer to, "How does Bilbo learn?" is that he learns from a stance of vulnerability. There is no sensation of being ready. "Ready" implies that one already knows and has prepared for what is to come. Learning demands facing what is to come as a novice, of being ready to learn without yet being ready to face the challenges that will result in the learning. For that reason, Gandalf is needed to rescue the travelers in their first challenges. Also for that reason, Bilbo meets his own first challenge in the pit of a cave, grasping around in the dark for a ring whose power he does not yet understand, and exchanging improvized riddles with a creature for whom riddles are only a bit more interesting at the time than eating the riddler. His first learning outcomes are motivated by mere survival.

However, Bilbo learns fast and applies what he is learning to immediately pressing situations. He reacts and adapts. As he does so, he builds his skill and knowledge repertoire, as well as his confidence to face the next encounter. As his confidence grows, so also do his senses of purpose and scope, with behaviors expanding to strategies, and strategies for physical outcomes expanding to strategies for social and ethical outcomes.

Along the way, Bilbo also learns by enjoying being praised and appreciated, not by an external evaluator but rather by the beneficiaries of, even collaborators in, his work. He learns as well by remaining humble, seeing his flaws and mistakes as teachers, not failures, with the humility arising from this awareness serving as a reminder that there is always room to improve and something new to learn. He is aware, in other words, that he will probably always leave the house in a hurry, unprepared for what may come, and open to discovering new ways to engage with each new experience. Why? Because another way that Bilbo learns is through trusting that his mentor (in this case, Gandalf, but this is a teacher's role in any example of Environmental Inquiry) is never too far away. Gandalf is more than willing to leave Bilbo to face his own challenges, always ready to offer the hobbit reassurances, public support, and praise, and ever available with his greater knowledge to let the hobbit watch from a nearby hilltop when the battle requires more than the student is yet able to bring to it.

Finally, Bilbo learns by giving himself a variety of opportunities to remember his lessons, and to reflect on and understand them with increasing depth. Retelling the stories of his adventures both orally along the way home, and in writing over the years that follow his return, Bilbo owns his experiences and the lessons they have brought him. Telling of them, writing them down in his own voice, his own narrative, allows him not only to rehearse and therefore to remember them, but also to return to them as he matures with greater and greater appreciation for their contributions to his lifespan. Meanwhile, finishing his education with a memoir, Bilbo seems to take on the role of scholar and teacher, leaving a written record for others who may become curious about a hobbit who felt a bit Tookish—an especially important document, I suspect, for young hobbits already feeling a bit Tookish, themselves. In his final educational act, therefore, Bilbo inspires and empowers future generations of learners who may be interested in, if not entirely ready for, their own hobbit's holiday.

NOTES

1. George Hillocks, Jr., *Research on Written Composition* (Urbana, IL: ERIC Clearinghouse on Reading and Communication Skills, 1986).

2. Ibid.

3. George Hillocks, Jr., *Teaching Writing as Reflective Practice* (New York: Teachers College Press, 1995).

4. Maria Montessori, *The Absorbent Mind* (New York: Holt, Rinehart, and Winston, 1967).

5. Ibid.

6. J. R. R. Tolkien, *The Hobbit* (New York: Ballantine Books, 1982), 1.

7. Ibid.

8. Ibid., 15.

9. Ibid., 19.

10. Ibid., 78.

11. Ibid.

12. Ibid., 79.

13. Ibid., 143.

14. Ibid., 180.

15. Ibid., 209.

16. Ibid.

17. Ibid., 211.

18. Ibid., 216.

19. Ibid., 223.

20. Ibid., 227.

21. Ibid., 235.

22. Ibid., 237.

23. Ibid.

24. Ibid.

25. Ibid., 269.

26. Ibid., 272.

27. Ibid.

28. Ibid., 273.

29. Ibid.

30. Ibid.

31. Ibid.

32. Ibid., 274.

33. Ibid., 277.

34. Ibid., 287.

35. Ibid., 290.

36. Ibid.

37. Ibid.

38. Ibid.

39. Ibid., 302.

40. Ibid., 304.

41. Ibid., 305.

42. Ibid.

Chapter 8

How Hogwarts Teaches

Identity, Personality, and Instruction

INTRODUCTION

How does Hogwarts teach? Pretty much exactly the way every school teaches, which is to say, in as many different ways as there are teachers on the faculty. The nature of that variety has been explored across several different bodies of research in and theory about pedagogy. As I mentioned earlier, Hillocks' meta-analysis revealed a sort of gravitational pull toward three modes of instruction. The mode that a teacher prefers appears to align with that teacher's ideological preferences.[1] For example, one method (naturalistic) might appeal to instructors naturally drawn to open-ended instructional styles which facilitate free response and empower students, while another (say, presentational) might appeal to one more strongly influenced by teachers of his or her past who used that same approach or who value knowledge transference as a learning outcome. Studies extending from that meta-analysis discovered personalized complications of this pedagogical array, suggesting that different teachers teach in different ways often simply by virtue of the uniqueness of the life they bring to the classroom. Likewise, methods range far beyond those categories in the meta-analysis, from the predictably traditional to the idiosyncratic and downright eccentric.[2]

Other researchers have found that the variable of personality appears strongly to influence not only how students prefer to learn, but also how teachers prefer to teach (and more importantly, those teachers' blind spots regarding their perceptions of what works and what their students need). In those cases, a teacher may be teaching as an expression of his or her own personality preferences, connecting amazingly well with students of similar preferences, but completely missing those students whose personality connects far better with other methods.[3] For example, a teacher of the tradition mentioned earlier who exclusively lectures may never truly appeal to the student who has to talk about information before ever fully comprehending it. Likewise, a teacher whose preference is for unstructured, open-ended, student-centered activities may never truly connect with the student who prefers structure and order, pre-determined outcomes and a clearly stated agenda.[4]

This research tradition, and the definition and measure of personality it is based on, is built on the work of psychologist Carl Jung. Jung's study of archetypes explores some of the sources of personal differences which become manifest on a regular basis, consciously and intentionally or not, through dreams, art, and stories, all in the language of ancient symbols which he traced throughout history and across cultures.[5] These images, Jung posited, and the various qualities that they represent, inform behavior and guide interactions, reflecting the forces and traits that make each of us most uniquely ourselves. Joseph Campbell translated Jung's ideas into a definition of the heroic journey as portrayed in ancient myths,[6] and Carol Pearson modernized Campbell's work to articulate a pantheon of images that guide different stages of personal development, according to each person's journey to become the hero of his or her own myth, which is to say his or her own life.[7] Applied to teaching, these figures argue that each person in charge of a classroom is guided by, and expresses, a system of values and identity that is unique and fully (though largely unconsciously) influential over his or her unique performance (whether planning or improvising, whether determining whom to call on or how to evaluate that person's response). Another popular and personalized version of this phenomenon is simply that we teach who we are.[8] Parker Palmer's work on teaching explores what he sees as the natural and (when teaching is at its best) intentional, open, and necessary connection between how people teach and there very personhood—their identity, values, personality, and interpersonal style, whether these traits are measured objectively or the sheer by-product of intrapersonal awareness.[9]

Shaped by any of these conceptual frameworks, the message is consistent—everybody is different, to the very core, and teachers are no exception. Furthermore, those differences are so powerful in driving our decisions and actions that even two people attempting to implement the same plan, and who report later that they have successfully done so, will show in their practice two completely different examples of classroom teaching. So, how does Hogwarts teach? Well, they have a pretty large faculty, with a peculiar element of turnover, and the reader starts meeting teachers long before arriving for the first day of class.

THE READING

First, in deference to the Harry Potter fans and aficionados who may be reading this, note that I only consider the first three novels in the series. I made something of an executive decision that those three would provide me with the most essential array of teachers, providing some degree of breadth and depth, without becoming its own book length project. I presume no fandom-level expertise in the overall narrative, just an educator's interest in its central imagery of school and teaching.

So, turning to the very first novel, to identify the very first teacher, allow me to introduce for pedagogical analysis, Mr. Dursley. That's right. Of course, I know that Mr. Dursley isn't by trade a classroom teacher, and he's certainly not on the faculty of Hogwarts, but I want to use him as a baseline, an illustration of "what not to do." Why even call him a teacher at all? Because he does have an educational agenda—to raise his family. It just so happens in this case that his family forms a classroom, if you will, with only two students. Dudley is the classic teacher's pet, and Harry is the classic "problem student." As it often occurs even in actual classrooms, this division is based not on merit but on bias. Dudley's privilege isn't earned, nor is Harry's suffering the result of any behavior that warrants remediation. This bias simply determines how the "teacher" perceives, defines, and reacts to the respective students. Its source is his bias against the kind of child Harry Potter is, the son of a mixed marriage of a normal human, or "muggle," and a wizard. In Mr. Dursley's "academy" wizardry is as unacceptable as (for some overly rigid, traditional classroom teachers) questioning authority, writing a six-paragraph theme, or starting a sentence with "and." In Mr. Dursley's "academy" wizardry is as suspect as it was for a child to be African American in the earliest years of school desegregation, as unworkable as it was for a child to have Down's Syndrome or autism in the years before behavioral science and public policy affirmed and normalized how human and teachable those children are, and how much others benefit from studying alongside them. In the case of Dursley and Potter, the teacher and the student come from different cultures, and (much as with early programs for Native Americans) the teacher is excessively vigilant about squashing any opportunity for the appearance (much less validation or exercise) of the student's culture.

Mr. Dursley doesn't make Harry sit in a corner wearing the iconic "dunce cap," or write punishment sentences, or call on him only for the purpose of inflicting public abuse, but the overall effect is similar. Harry is relegated to his cupboard under the stairs and forbidden to mention most of the characteristics that make him unique and powerful. The first of Harry's' visitors from Hogwarts are Albus Dumbledore and Professor McGonagall.

They arrive secretly to confirm Harry's identity and to provide the reader the first summary of the boy's back story. The second visitors from Hogwarts arrive in the form of letters that assault the house, letters that actively reach out from the wizard's school recruiting Harry's attendance. They come in such larger and larger quantities and at a greater and greater frequency that they chase the Dursley's, Harry included, away to a remote cottage on a small island on what happens to be Harry's birthday.

It is there that Harry receives his third contact from Hogwarts, a visit from one Rubeus Hagrid. And it is Hagrid who first establishes the contrast between that which Harry has so far been taught, and that which is his truth. Harry's initial ignorance is even expressed in terms of school knowledge. When Hagrid expresses angry astonishment at discovering that Harry, "' knows nothin' abou'—about ANYTHING . . . ,' Harry thought this was going a bit far. He had been to school, after all, and his marks weren't bad. 'I know *some* things,' he said. 'I can, you know, do math and stuff.'"[10] It is yet another contrast between traditional school content and those matters which will soon be presented as truly worth learning.

Note that from the outset of the first novel, Rowling's fictional educational message is one that not only will go on to honor the individual voices and gifts of its faculty, but see, honor, and nurture the unique identity of its students. Individuality, it may be said, is one of Hogwarts' core values. Hagrid certainly knows who Harry is, as do Dumbledore and McGonagall. If Dumbledore and McGonagall's first task on behalf of Hogwarts is to find and identify their newest star student, Hagrid's is to manage the logistics of getting that student to school. Once all of the new students have arrived and been sorted into their appropriate houses, Rowling provides her reader (in chapters eight and nine of *The Sorcerer's Stone*) with a survey of faculty personalities and teaching methods. I begin this chapter likewise. From there I will focus in more detail on the teachers who occupy a very specific niche on the faculty, all instructors in Defense Against the Dark Arts, a position that especially early on in the series is notably difficult to keep staffed. They are, in order of holding the position, Professors Quirrell, Lockhart, and Lupin. The final cluster of teachers examined in this chapter are the four who define instruction at the school and are in fact integral to life at Hogwarts across the entire narrative and across history within that narrative—Hagrid, McGonagall, Snape, and Dumbledore.

So, as a form of faculty roll call, and offered perhaps to establish Hogwarts as a real school, and not just a castle where a few eccentric characters live and do their magic, Rowling narrates: "And then . . . there were the classes themselves."[11] Herbology is taught by "a dumpy little witch called Professor Sprout."[12] The class is described simply as being, "where they learned how to take care of all the strange plants and fungi, and found out what they were used for."[13]

Professor Binns teaches History of Magic. "Easily the most boring class," the only truly interesting thing about Binns' class seems to be Binns' own story, which itself even includes a sort of meta-reference to boredom. Apparently, "Professor Binns had been very old indeed when he had fallen asleep in front of the staffroom fire and got up the next morning to teach, leaving his body behind him."[14] So, Binns died while napping, left his body, and continues teaching as a ghost. As such, in Binns' classroom History is reduced to droning lectures about names and dates, the likes of which he made more difficult to follow by mixing up. Perhaps Binns was planning his own lesson and bored himself to sleep as he sat by the fire.

Professor Flitwick is the Charms teacher. Flitwick first appears as, "a tiny little wizard who had to stand on a pile of books to see over his desk."[15] It is also noted in these first comments that he became very excited upon seeing Harry's name during roll call, a point that includes Flitwick among those aware of Harry's identity, and happy to have the new special student in his class.

The next three teachers in the initial review get significantly more attention later in this chapter. Professor McGonagall, whom we actually first meet in the form of a cat on Privet Drive, is introduced as a "different . . . strict and clever" kind of classroom teacher.[16] Then, we meet Quirrell, who teaches a class called Defense Against the Dark Arts. The first things readers learn about Quirrell is that, while everyone had been looking forward to his class, in reality, his teaching is "a bit of a joke."[17] His room has an offensive odor of garlic which implies an overactive concern about vampires, and in his first reported interaction with a student he dodges a question. The question reflects the student's enthusiasm; yet, it is met with the kind of change of subject indicating that the teacher has no valid answer, and implicitly no expertise. In short, instead of answering the students question Quirrell, "went pink and started talking about the weather."[18]

Finishing out the faculty introductions is Potions instructor, Professor Snape. Snape first appears via reference as the children are talking over breakfast about their day's classes. "'Double Potions with the Slytherins,' said Ron. 'Snape's Head of Slytherin House. They say he always favors them—we'll be able to see if it's true."[19] So, this teacher is the head of one of the school's houses, and he seems to play favorites. It remains to be seen if that rumor plays out in Snape's actual instruction.

Snape's first action in the classroom is to take roll. Arriving at Harry's name causes him to pause, much as did Flitwick, but not with the same squealing excitement. Instead, Snape announces, "Harry Potter. Our new—*celebrity*."[20]

The sign that Snape's intention is sarcastic, not respectful or excited, is that the students from his house, "sniggered behind their hands."[21] Another suggestion of Snape's personality comes in the description of his very face: "His eyes . . . were cold and empty and made you think of dark tunnels."[22] His earliest teaching methods include a combination of silence, detailed commentary on the importance, rarity, and potential danger of his subject matter, and a knack for asking questions designed more to intimidate and reveal weakness than to engage or challenge or validate learning. He singles out Harry to pursue with questions he already knows Harry can't answer, and then ignores Hermione's enthusiastically raised hand.

Snape does ultimately provide answers to his own questions in ways that educate, but he does so by pointing out many of his students' (not just Harry's) inadequacy to answer the questions themselves, going so far as to call the student, Neville, "Idiot boy!"[23] for failing to add porcupine quills in the right order when mixing them into a potion. In his defense, however, this anger is sparked when Neville has already begun to show symptoms of this mistake: "angry red boils sprang up all over his arms and legs . . . [and] . . . started to pop up all over his nose."[24] It could as easily be that Snape's anger is directed not at students he dislikes, but behavior he deems destructive to their well-being, or to the craft he is attempting to teach. What will emerge as Snape's larger instructional method and educational effect may be generalized as, "tough love." He often acts with the students' and school's best interest at heart, while doing so in a brutal or cynical way. Even his favoritism could be argued to be educational, given that it isn't something he hides, and it mainly creates the conditions that motivate students from other houses to earn what they are awarded.

Last of the general introductions, Madame Hooch is the instructor for riding broomsticks, a skill not only essential for functioning traditionally as a witch, but also for playing the school's main sporting event, Quidditch. Madame Hooch, like many coaches and instructors of physical education, has the advantage of working within a field that, unlike perhaps that of her colleague Professor Binns, lends itself well to experiential learning. In her first scene, she guides her students through a demonstration and subsequent practice session of broomstick usage. This trait of her material adds a certain urgency to her instruction, as she sternly calls her class to a carefully sequenced action. Step one, the command to make the broomstick rise from the ground into the student's hand, step two the proper stance for mounting the broom, and step three instructions for rising on the broomstick into the air.

When her student, (again, alas!) Neville, fails in properly executing her instructions, pushing off from the ground nervously and prematurely, and falling from his broomstick so hard that he breaks his wrist, Madame Hooch assesses his injury and walks him to the school hospital for attention. As she leaves, her instructions about restraint are as clear and direct as had been her instruction about participation: "You leave those brooms where they are or you'll be out of Hogwarts before you can say, 'Quidditch.'"[25]

So the style of teaching at Hogwarts ranges across a familiar variety of teacher stereotypes: the boring eccentric, the aloof intimidator, the friendly bumbler, the assertive authority figure, the insightful sage. Now, for a deeper dive into the lives of three professors assigned consecutively to teach the same class: Defense Against the Dark Arts. Appearing in the first novel, Professor Quirrell meets Harry even before the students arrive at Hogwarts. As Harry is shopping for school supplies with Hagrid in Diagon Alley, "A pale young man made his way forward, very nervously. One of his eyes was twitching."[26] Quirrell arrives in the narrative as a polite and welcoming teacher with a noticeable speech impediment, a nervous laugh, and an open fear of vampires. When Harry asks Hagrid about the new teacher, the latter explains that while Quirrell is a master of the textbook side of his craft, "he met vampires in the Black Forest, and there was a nasty bit o' trouble with a hag—never been the same since. Scared of the students, scared of his own subject."[27]

In the classroom, as outlined above, Quirrell is a disappointment, lacking both personal appeal (the garlic he uses presumably is intended to manage his phobia of vampires) and intellectual authority (he dodges student questions in favor of nervous small talk). Even around school, he is nervous, weak, fearful, and prone to panic. It is Quirrell who appears in the door to the dining hall to announce the attack of a troll, but "He then sank to the floor in a dead faint."[28] At the scene of the troll's demise, McGonagall and Snape work to settle the matter and get things back to normal for the students, but useless Quirrell only feigns a heart attack. The first suggestion that there is more than meets the reader's eye with Quirrell is the description of a meeting that Harry overhears between Quirrell and Snape. Snape is attempting to devise a way to get past the beast who is guarding the Sorcerer's Stone, and he turns to Quirrell for help. Quirrell attempts to deflect Snape's request by feigning ignorance of the whole situation, but the Potions teacher challenges, "You know perfectly well what I mean,"[29] implying that Snape knows perfectly well what Quirrell knows.

The children believe that Snape is trying to get Quirrell to use his knowledge of Dark Arts to help him get the stone. What they don't consider is that Snape is not the one to fear. That point becomes clear near the end of the novel as Harry approaches the character whom he is convinced is his main adversary, only to find out that, "it wasn't Snape. It wasn't even Voldemort. It was Quirrell."[30] In this confrontation, Quirrell has stopped trembling, twitching, and stuttering. He speaks calmly, as he explains to Harry how it was never Snape who was fighting against him, but rather "p-p-poor, st-stuttering

P-Professor Quirrell," hiding behind Snape's image of aggression.[31] Quirrell has been pretending all along to be weak and fragile, so as to do Voldemort's bidding against Harry. However, Quirrell's deception runs far beyond hiding his evil reality behind a weak persona, he is actually a literal host for Voldemort, a living entity hiding as an attachment to Quirrell's head and covered by his ever-present, ever-smelly turban.

Considering Quirrell as a model of teaching, his dishonesty and manipulation become the most visible traits. Professor Quirrell pretends to be weak in order to accomplish an evil and destructive agenda without being considered strong enough to be the likely culprit. Furthermore, his agenda isn't his own, but rather belongs to the force of evil within whose grip he has fallen. Weak even within his position of power, Quirrell represents the kind of teacher who blindly implements a school or curricular agenda, not for the collegiality it earns him among fellow teachers or the achievement it nurtures for students, but merely for the favor it gains him from an administrator. He is also the kind of teacher who will never own up to this operation, because its success depends precisely on his duplicity.

In the next novel, *Harry Potter and the Chamber of Secrets*, Gilderoy Lockhart replaces Quirrell as Professor of Defense Against the Dark Arts. While Lockhart is not an ally and pawn of Voldemort, his duplicity operates as strongly over his instructional performance. While Quirrell uses deception to gain power without being suspected of its destruction, Lockhart uses deception to feel a degree of power he doesn't actually possess. Even though Lockhart pretends to be a heroic scholar, writer, and teacher, his skills don't back up his image, and his teaching only confirms his own ineptitude.

Coincidentally, just as with Quirrell, Lockhart's first appearance in the narrative is in Diagon Alley, when Harry walks up on Lockhart's book signing for his memoir. The egocentric Lockhart begins:

> "When young Harry here stepped into Flourish and Blotts today, he only wanted to buy my new autobiography—which I shall be happy to present him now, free of charge . . . . He had no idea . . . that he would shortly be getting much, much more than my book, *Magical Me*. He and his schoolmates will, in fact, be getting the real magical me. Yes, ladies and gentlemen, I have great pleasure and pride in announcing that this September, I will be taking up the post of Defense Against the Dark Arts teacher at Hogwarts School of Witchcraft and Wizardry!" The crowd cheered and clapped and Harry found himself being presented with the entire works of Gilderoy Lockhart.[32]

They have a more private meeting once school has begun, as Lockhart pulls Harry aside in the hallway outside Professor Sprout's classroom. Lockhart attempts to follow up on what he assesses to be Harry's need for publicity (since that would be Lockhart's own motive under similar circumstances), as exhibited (in Lockhart's assessment) by the boy's landing the car dramatically in the Womping Willow. Presuming empathy and insight into Harry's motives, Lockhart more realistically attempts to form an alliance with Harry, validating his own egotism by piggy-backing Harry's authentic reputation.

In his own classroom, Lockhart proves that his own largely self-authored publicity is mere hype. Classroom activities quickly descend into chaos, as the professor begins with a flourish of self-promotion, followed by a fifty-four-item quiz consisting exclusively of questions about himself and a word of reassurance (once actual instruction is imminent) that "no harm can befall you whilst I am here,"[33] and culminating shortly thereafter with the unleashing of a group of pixies over which he has absolutely no control and as a result of which, "It was pandemonium":

> The pixies shot in every direction like rockets. Two of them seized Neville by the ears and lifted him into the air. Several shot straight through the window, showering the back row with broken glass. The rest proceeded to wreck the classroom more effectively than a rampaging rhino.[34]

Once the professor finally steps in to exert some kind of authority over the "pandemonium" he had unleashed, his efforts seem initially confident and promising: "He rolled up his sleeves, brandished his wand, and bellowed, *'Peskipiksi Pesternomi!'*" Alas, "It had absolutely no effect."[35] Gilderoy Lockhart, so it would seem, can neither practice nor teach in the area in which he is assigned and publicly lauded.

The sham that is Quirrell is the illusion of inept innocence. The sham that is Lockhart is the illusion of excellence (or even competence). What quality of deception may define Lockhart's successor, the third instructor to conduct classes in The Defense Against the Dark Arts, Professor Lupin?

In his first appearance, Lupin, unlike his predecessors, is not wandering around Diagon Alley but rather hiding in plain sight (his particular brand of duplicity?). He is the mysterious occupant of a train car on the Hogwarts Express, as Ron, Harry, and Hermione are looking for a seat. He is described as a "stranger . . . wearing an extremely shabby set of wizard's robes that had been darned in several places. He looked ill and exhausted. Though quite young, his light brown hair was flecked with gray."[36] The children identify him by the name Professor R. J. Lupin stamped on "a small, battered case held together with a large quantity of neatly knotted string."[37]

Dumbledore offers the school a more formal introduction of Professor Lupin, "who had kindly consented," he explains, "to fill the post of Defense Against the Dark Arts teacher."[38] The narrator notes that "Professor Lupin looked particularly shabby next to all the other teachers in their best robes."[39]

As first impressions go, therefore, Lupin's is the opposite of Lockhart's gaudy show, and calmer than Quirrell's nervous pretense of ineptness. The children automatically like him, and on the first day of class his methods prove to be far more experiential (the word he uses, is "practical") than academic. After instructing them to put their books back into their book bags, Lupin invites them to follow him out, two gestures reminiscent of various fictional teachers (among the most famous being Mr. Keating from, *Dead Poets' Society*) whose respective stories mark them as especially innovative and inspiring. In Lupin's case, students follow him into the hallway, not (as with Keating) to a trophy case, but rather to an encounter with Peeves the Poltergiest, "who was floating upside down in midair and stuffing the nearest keyhole with chewing gum."[40] Unlike a similar moment with his predecessor, Lupin was unfazed by Peeves' teasing, and when the Poltergeist resisted Lupin's command, the professor "gave a small sigh and took out his wand. 'This is a useful little spell,' he told the class over his shoulder. 'Please watch closely.'"[41] The ease and immediacy with which the teacher's demonstration worked impresses a student, who proclaimed that act, "cool." The apparently egoless Lupin simply thanks the student, puts away his wand, and asks, "Shall we proceed?"[42]

Lupin leads the students farther down the hall into the staff room, within which there is a wardrobe visibly and audibly rattling with a shape-shifter called a Boggart. In order to teach his lesson on the Boggart, Lupin first selects his meekest student, (yet again) Neville Longbottom. In a constructive twist on the role Neville has played thus far, Lupin states, "I am sure he will perform . . . admirably."[43] Then, Lupin shows his own expert knowledge of the shape-shifter, explaining what it is and how it operates. After this introduction, Lupin begins the "academic" portion of the lesson, helping the students identify the actual traits of a Boggart, a task at which Hermione (whose strength is academics) excels. This portion of the lesson leads them to identify a way to use specific knowledge about the Boggart in order to encounter it relatively safely. Simply put, the Boggart becomes whatever the person encountering it most fears; with more people in the encounter, the Boggart becomes confused as to which fear to manifest; thus, Lupin has created a safe lesson based on his high-level content knowledge of the subject's risk. Furthermore, he guides his students through these stages of reasoning not via lecturing about it to them, but via experience and discussion, whereby students receive not only Lupin's information, but also follow (and participate in) his reasoning.

As a final point, Lupin shares the truly secret weapon that "really finishes" a Boggart, laughter: "What you need to do is force it to assume a shape that you find amusing."[44] But the lesson, itself, is only beginning, as is its involvement of the unsure and unlikely chosen-student-leader mentioned earlier, Neville. One by one, beginning with Neville, each student first identifies that which he or she is most afraid (in Neville's case, it is Professor Snape). The student then imagines that figure in a comical state (Neville pictures Snape dressed as the boy's grandmother). When that version of the boggart materializes, the reaction is laughter instead of fear, thus disorienting the boggart. As each student at Lupin's invitation takes a turn, each offering yet another confusion, the boggart is ultimately Neville's to "finish off." "This time Neville charged forward looking determined. *'Riddikulus!'* he shouted, and they had a split second's view of Snape in his lacy dress before Neville let out a great 'Ha!' of laughter, and the boggart exploded, burst into a thousand tiny wisps of smoke, and was gone."[45]

In summary, Lupin teaches content knowledge, but he also teaches the processes of inquiry as well as those required for achievement. Perhaps most important of all, he nurtures courage and (by extension) confidence in the attempt. I should add that the one student who does not attempt to trick the boggart during Lupin's lesson is Harry. This detail of Lupin's lesson puzzles Harry more than it seems to affect Lupin. The teacher in this case is well aware of the magnitude of his student's fear, and is comfortably willing to differentiate his approach to accommodate Harry's unusual situation. "Professor Lupin had deliberately stopped him from tackling the boggart," because he knew there was no way for Harry to render his worst fear into a harmless form.[46] Lupin knows the difference between a banshee, a giant spider, or even Professor Snape, and Lord Voldemort. His judgment as a teacher in that instructional moment contributes partly to maintaining order and safety in his "classroom" (a skill that his immediate predecessor sorely lacked) and also to protect the safety of his unique student, Harry.

Professor Lupin ultimately becomes yet the third teacher of The Defense Against the Dark Arts to leave after a single year, but not in this case because he is inept in the classroom or morally corrupt in character. Lupin's departure becomes the only way for him to manage a trait that accounts for his great sensitivity and intuition, even as it becomes his one great secret and the source of his earlier mentioned duplicity. Professor Lupin is a werewolf, and the recurrences of this form make normal life increasingly difficult to maintain. In that sense, he fits in alongside many of the teachers portrayed across film and literature as "great." That which makes him special, makes him especially effective, but also especially dangerous and fragile. Think of the archetypes of the heroic teacher over the years—the brilliant iconoclast, selfless to the point of self-destructive, insightful to the point of rebellious, yet trying to fit in and keep his job. Only three great teachers manage to remain on the Hogwarts faculty for their entire careers (four if you count Hagrid, which I do). Consequently, I will begin with the gentle giant and then work my way toward this chapter's conclusion through Professors Snape, McGonagall, and Dumbledore.

An entirely separate book could be written about this group of literary pedagogues. Consequently, I will reiterate my original disclaimer and apologize to anyone looking here for a detailed analysis either of the characters as beloved icons or examples of their teaching practices across the entire series. In fact, to help maintain my focus even from the tendency to sort through endless passages which may illustrate particular moments of instruction, I will sort these four Hogwarts teachers by the iconic qualities of personal character that I perceive drive their instruction, beginning with Hagrid, a teacher guided by his Heart.

Long before the title character even knows about Hogwarts, Hagrid emotionally delivers the baby Harry Potter to the dubious safety of Privet Drive, and upon his return he warmly wishes Harry a happy twelfth birthday. He's the one who annually ushers all of the children through their preparations in Diagon Alley and onto the Hogwarts Express along the way of their return to each next school year. He is the archetypal former student, whose love for the school—for its ways and history, its faculty, and especially its students—has kept him in that school's employ living in a hut on the grounds and serving its various needs for care, love, and emotional support. Enhancing his nurturing image is Hagrid's affinity for all creatures in and around Hogwarts. For example, he shares his house with a boarhound named Fang. Then, when Harry asks later about the animal guarding the Chamber of Secrets, Hagrid indicates that he already is quite familiar with the three-headed dog, Fluffy. This dog also belongs to Hagrid, his having loaned the beast out to Dumbledore for the very purpose of guarding the Chamber. Further, it is Hagrid who raises his beloved Norwegian Ridgeback dragon, Norbert, from an egg into hatchling, and refers to himself as he cares for Norbert, as "his mummy!"[47]

But as a teacher, as with many teachers of this strength, Hagrid's heart is sometimes too big and warm to be effective at the more strategic aspects of classroom instruction. He is too permissive to be a good disciplinarian. His love both for his animals and the children in his charge prompts fear, panic, and self-loathing at least as often as it prompts effective action. On several occasions, it is through their efforts to help Hagrid, not through his efforts to help them, that his students learn the most consequential lessons. But they do rise to the challenge of helping him, because they know the depth and breadth of his love for them and the school.

The teacher driven by an expression of the heart builds the kinds of relationships that often overcome isolated mistakes and missteps. Hagrid's most important form of teaching is through his individual, private guidance usually offered in response to the students approaching him with questions or requests for his uniquely acquired insider information. That information, itself, gathered over Hagrid's years at the school, is a sort of instructional content built not by scholarship but by personal experience and awareness of institutional nuance.

When Hagrid actually gets some instructional time in Care of Magical Creatures class, he begins by attempting to introduce his students to the deep respect for and knowledge of the particular creature of that day's lesson, Buckbeak the hippogriff. The greater degree to which Hagrid's students follow his directions and emulate his empathy, the greater success they have in approaching and even riding Buckbeak. It is only when Draco Malfoy defies these rules of respect and empathy, denying Buckbeak's potential danger and calling him a "great ugly brute," that the lesson immediately turns bloody and chaotic.[48] Friends of Draco all blame Hagrid, but Harry, Ron, and Hermione know better. What they witness is a lesson in heart, delivered in trust, that goes unheeded by students not ready for that level of responsibility.

Professor Snape is a teacher guided by what I identify as Sacrifice. It is not the sacrifice typically associated with the term—putting others' needs before one's own, generosity to a fault, even popular images of martyrdom. Snape's sacrifice (and this fits my reading of Slytherins' brand of virtue in general) is a giving up of baser impulses for the good of a larger cause. Snape (or, again, any of the best that comes of Slytherin House) also knows how to sacrifice a level of potentially naïve vulnerability in order to see clearly the elements of the world that are best viewed skeptically. He sneers at Harry's fame, knowing that there is more to success than one's reputation (an insight that might have served the good Professor Lockhart well). Snape is loyal to Hogwarts without enjoying much (or perhaps any) public recognition for being so. As a member of the faculty, Snape accepts his role as that necessary figure who is willing to be unpopular in order to keep students sharp who otherwise would (as they do Hagrid) take advantage of the effects of "flattery" and admiration. Those forces don't work on Snape, and he emphasizes that point by dishing out doubt and disapproval even before a student might think he cares about being popular.

As a classroom instructor, Snape's first interaction with Harry is a question. Harry considers the question and falters. Snape replies smugly, but also with a sort of wisdom regarding Harry's legitimate learning challenge, "fame clearly isn't everything.'"[49] The interaction continues along a similar line as Snape asks more questions, each of which Hermione has an answer, but none of which prompts anything but more, "I don't know's" from Harry. This sequence seems like a singular agenda to torment and publically humiliate Harry, but it is just as much a lesson for Hermione about her own variation of stardom (the know-it-all). After the exercise in dual humility, Snape explains the subject matter that, on one hand, Harry hadn't studied, and that on the other, Hermione had planned to use as a means of gaining praise or perhaps simply to show off.

Another revealing and deceptively complex moment of Snape's actions as a teacher comes as he is seen murmuring incantations during Harry's frightening loss of control while flying in his first Quidditch match. It is assumed throughout most of the novel that Snape had caused the incident as a way to throw the match to Slytherin and punish the boy whom he appears so to hate. Hagrid (the Heart) knows better even in the moment, understanding intuitively that regardless of Snape's personality he would never do anything to intentionally harm a student. However, it isn't until the very end of the novel, in a narrative debriefing of sorts with Dumbledore, that Harry realizes that not only was Snape not causing the trouble but was actually offering counterspells to keep Harry safe from Quirrell's incantations.

True to type, however, Snape's work should not be seen as pure and simple, Hagrid-like goodwill. As Dumbledore explains, "he worked so hard to protect you this year because he felt that would make him and your father even."[50] A temporary sacrifice of his baser impulses, hatred, serves a larger cause, honor, ultimately in service of yet another a base impulse, guilt-free resentment—which means that Snape holds honor in higher esteem than resentment and hatred. Virtue, the Slytherin way. As an image of teaching, Snape prioritizes what students need and what he can offer as skill and expertise over whatever he may feel about students personally, which is a perennially constructive trait among teachers working every day with children who are their own worst enemies, or who defiantly resist teachers' efforts, or who disrespect their own capacity to learn.

What Snape accomplishes in this context through Sacrifice, Professor McGonagall accomplishes through the more neutral force of Justice. As mentioned earlier, Minerva McGonagall is one of the first two faculty members to see young Harry. She and Professor Dumbledore are both there in the Dursley's neighborhood the night Hagrid delivers the sleeping baby to his aunt and uncle's for safekeeping. The next time Harry sees her, Professor McGonagall is standing at the top of the Hogwart's main stairway greeting the newest incoming students. She ushers them to the Great Hall where they will be sorted into houses before the start-of-term banquet. Throughout this process, McGonagall functions as curator and monitor of procedures. She directs the students to the proper places, explains purposes, traditions, and the evening's schedule, and as such she keeps events and people moving along smoothly. In the classroom, she was, "strict and clever," and "gave them a talking to the moment they sat down."[51] Around the school, it is Professor McGonagall who regularly doles out the points and demerits, as members of one house or another behave honorably, violate rules, or take risks that warrant judgment calls, prompting both reprimand and reconsideration, punishments and second chances.

She even knows well how to navigate the nuanced, personal particulars of a problem behind the public impression of judicious appearances. On more than one occasion, she pulls Harry aside to solicit his help after just reprimanding him for what appeared publically to be his role in the problem. In this respect, she offers a shade of her colleague, Professor Snape, often working for a higher good by departing from her official persona. That persona, and its guiding power of justice, simply happens already to position McGonagall in a more egalitarian public role. Few students who are punished by McGonagall suspect her of favoritism or cruelty, and consequently few have to look past her behavior for the pursuit of the good. And yet, she uses this reputation to pursue deeper levels of good, much as does her colleague, Hagrid, through private conversations that students learn to trust as valid variations of her formal, judicial agenda.

But no one on the Hogwarts faculty uses individual encounters more effectively than Professor Dumbledore. One-on-one lessons are his stock in trade. That is because his teaching is driven by a force most clearly suited for the case-by-case, as-needed, teachable moment—Wisdom. It is the wise teacher who knows enough to recognize when a lesson is needed, and when a student is ready. It is with wisdom, and not just knowledge or training, that a teacher learns how to customize material for students' individual interests. Such teaching requires specific bits of knowledge as well as an awareness of how those bits fit into the bigger picture and apply to new situations. Likewise, such teaching is hardly ever appropriate for whole groups of students, but rather is best when offered to the very student whose circumstances require that very lesson.

In that capacity, Dumbledore provides his individual charges (primarily Harry) instruction in two main forms—tools and debriefing. By tools, I mean the various devices—maps, cloaks, fonts of magical elixir—which Harry uses either to see or move around, thereby gaining access and insights. Harry can learn not only about the past, but also about current relevant events at various locations in or around Hogwarts that reveal truths about his growing power as a wizard, and his constant effort to survive another day (or novel) to continue practicing that power. By "debriefing," I mean the recurring moments when, usually in Dumbledore's chambers, Harry's most recent trials are explained in the context of his past, the school's past, and their roles in his ongoing growth.

Dumbledore could always simply have explained those points of history or threat or resolution to Harry, but in each case, he prepares the young wizard for those explanations by guiding him (sometimes secretly, and sometimes explicitly) through his own direct experiences. Since the experiences always come first, usually via one of those specialized tools, and prompted by the discovery of a puzzle that urgently needs attention and requires action, the debriefing allows Harry to integrate authentically, though sometimes awkwardly, discovered fragments into a coherent whole. This "whole" is a learning outcome that students can't often see when receiving academic information in an experiential vacuum, but likewise can't often access experientially without specialized tools and expert guidance.

So, how *does* Hogwarts teach? As I mentioned at the very beginning of this chapter, it "teaches" in much the same way as any school. Some teachers lecture and put students to sleep. Some teachers are loveable, but a little inept. Some teachers seem really mean, but are in fact quite good. Some teachers seem quite nice, even weak, but are in fact quite destructive. Some teachers have an over-inflated sense of their own importance and ability. Some teachers are strict, yet understanding, while some teachers are permissive though never too far away to offer help. And some teachers are simply, calmly, steadily good. They engage their students, manage their materials, provide just the right amounts of support and allow just the right amounts of freedom. But, as with many schools, those very teachers are the ones who, for various reasons other than being a werewolf, leave the profession for pursuits that feel more true to their nature, or at least more accepting of their eccentricities.

As schools go, Hogwarts provides more experiential learning opportunities than most—probably because of its specific curricular emphases on magical practices—but similar schools with strong programs in career and technical education (auto mechanics, allied health, culinary arts, cosmetology) can point to similarly experiential curricula. Furthermore, many teachers of history, English, or math are especially effective because they find ways (as the cliché goes, though usually by a more mundane form of magic) to bring their material to life. Hogwarts also provides learning communities (in this case, Houses) that recognize differences across personality, disposition, and intellectual priorities, and the valuable contributions that can be made across those differences. Hufflepuffs build community and value fairness; Ravenclaws build intelligence especially through academic study; Slytherins build power that provides access to darker forces that otherwise might attack, corrupt, and destroy; and Gryffindors build strength through a combination of courage and virtue. But courage can be misplaced without the intelligence of the Ravenclaw or the fairness of Hufflepuff, and kindness (even virtue) can be misplaced without the knowledge of the evil and nefarious intentions so clear to the Slytherin.

The school structure at Hogwarts is set up to create something akin to a reverse version of a university's General Education Core. Instead of a core curriculum that everyone takes to form a foundation for diving more deeply (and vocationally) into their major, the curriculum at Hogwarts is designed to provide an intensive education in the vocation of wizardry, with an organizational structure, which channels that education out into the variety of personalities (sorted into their houses) of those who will be practicing it. The faculty there reflects much of that same kind of variety. Thus, a graduate of Hogwarts will have learned to practice wizardry in a way that most expresses his or her nature, mind, and personality, from a faculty busily being themselves, practicing their own respective nature, mind, and personality. Sometimes, that prompts the occasional nap in history class. But sometimes, it means discovering that you're the hero of your own story.

NOTES

1. George Hillocks, Jr., *Research on Written Composition* (Urbana, IL: ERIC Clearinghouse on Reading and Communication Skills, 1986).

2. George Hillocks, Jr., *Ways of Thinking, Ways of Teaching* (New York: Teachers College Press, 1999).

3. George Jensen and John K. DiTiberio, *Personality and the Teaching of Composition* (New York: Ablex Corporation, 1989).

4. Ibid.

5. Carl Jung, *Memories, Dreams, Reflections* (New York: Vintage Books, 1989).

6. Joseph Campbell, *The Hero With a Thousand Faces* (New York: Pantheon Books, 1949).

7. Carol Pearson, *The Hero Within: Six Archetypes We Live By* (New York: HarperOne, 1986).

8. Parker Palmer, *The Courage to Teach* (San Francisco: Jossey-Bass, 2007).

9. Ibid.

10. J. K. Rowling, *Harry Potter and the Sorcerer's Stone* (New York: Scholastic, 1999), 49.

11. Ibid., 133.

12. Ibid.

13. Ibid.

14. Ibid.

15. Ibid.

16. Ibid.

17. Ibid., 134.

18. Ibid.

19. Ibid., 135.

20. Ibid., 136.

21. Ibid.

22. Ibid.

23. Ibid., 139.

24. Ibid.

25. Ibid., 147.

26. Ibid., 70.

27. Ibid., 70–71.

28. Ibid., 172.

29. Ibid., 226.

30. Ibid., 287–288.

31. Ibid., 288.

32. J. K. Rowling, *Harry Potter and the Chamber of Secrets* (New York: Scholastic, 2000), 60–61.

33. Ibid., 101.

34. Ibid., 102.

35. Ibid.

36. J. K. Rowling, *Harry Potter and the Prisoner of Azkaban* (New York: Scholastic, 2001), 74.

37. Ibid.

38. Ibid., 92.

39. Ibid.

40. Ibid., 131.

41. Ibid.

42. Ibid.

43. Ibid., 132.

44. Ibid., 134.

45. Ibid., 139.

46. Ibid.

47. J. K. Rowling, *Harry Potter and the Sorcerer's Stone* (New York: Scholastic, 1999), 235.

48. J. K. Rowling, *Harry Potter and the Prisoner of Azkaban* (New York: Scholastic, 2001), 118.

49. J. K. Rowling, *Harry Potter and the Sorcerer's Stone* (New York: Scholastic, 1999), 137.

50. Ibid., 300.

51. Ibid., 133.

Epilogue

Lessons in Literature: What Readers See Through the Lens of Education

In hindsight, it isn't surprising that much of British children's literature offers images of and ideas about education. As a group, with Rowling as perhaps the one notable exception, these authors' class and privilege offered them access to England's most highly respected schools. At least three of the genre's most famous authors (Carroll/Dodgson, Lewis, and Tolkien) weren't just well-educated. They were themselves faculty members at Oxford, with first-hand experience of the education process and the halls in which some of the world's most valued education still flourishes. What *is* surprising is that one prevailing theme across the narratives is a cynicism toward formal education.

In the very opening lines, Alice is being bored to nearly catatonic lethargy as her sister reads a school book, which is disappointingly lacking in "pictures or conversations," the most reliable indicators of life, voice, and personality. Even after she is aroused by her sighting of the white rabbit, Alice's own most recent classroom education is quickly revealed as rote, superficial, merely performative and utterly useless as she falls down the rabbit hole grasping (metaphorically) at fragments of information that may explain what she is experiencing. Hers is a story of gradually letting go of the lessons she has been taught in school, and trusting the growing body of intelligence and autonomy she is building through her experience, reason, and discourse in Wonderland and Looking-Glass House.

Alongside the ongoing criticism of formal education is the mockery of those who seem to support, even celebrate those traditions. Owl, for example, in the tales of Winnie-the-Pooh, or Mr. Toad in *The Wind in the Willows* are examples, but also Mr. Jeremy Fisher and his friends, Alderman Ptolemy and Sir Isaac Newton, or even the proud, diligent bookworm, Hermione Granger—these characters, each in his or her way, illustrate a danger in becoming so invested in the results of formal education that they create blind spots to experiential surprise or independent reflection and reasoning.

Caught between the imagery that cautions and that which celebrates formal education are those characters who have tried to comply with the tradition, and yet lead lives scarred by their loyalty. There is no clearer example of this educational outcome than Captain James Hook, the former Eton boy who never quite gained the favor of his classmates, never quite mastered the art of "good form," and never quite got over the pain of not measuring up to his school's expectations (or maybe it was his own expectations of what his school promised him he would become). The same could be said, though somewhat less dramatically, of Mr. Darling (who often stands as a "reality" based Hook counterpart in theatrical productions, with the same actor cast in both roles). While Mr. Darling's own education isn't as explicitly noted as is Captain Hook's, his insecurities about failing to meet expectations are every bit as significant. He enters the narrative in the play as one who is frantically trying to tie his tie, so as to succeed at impressing his co-workers and superiors at the dinner they are preparing to attend, lest he not be able to show his face at the office and, consequently, bring financial ruin to his family. This is the voice of one who is desperate to fulfill the promises of his preparation for his definition of adulthood. Peter Pan, by contrast, has completely abandoned any interest in growing up, thereby lingering in his own reactionary resentment of the very kind of establishment that fuels Hook's and Mr. Darling's desperation.

But Eeyore and Pooh, likewise, could be considered as candidates for the rank of wounded alumni, the former having learned to expect the worst of his efforts, and the latter (though as I explain, ultimately redeemed by his own patience) at times a walking personification of self-doubt, ever surprised by his own intelligence. For that matter, Harry Potter, though an immediate hero of his Hogwarts narrative, suffers for years ahead of his enrollment in Hogwarts School of Witchcraft and Wizardry as the Dursley's problem child. His plight on Privet Drive is not all that different from Hook's at Eton, though Harry's efforts lead him more quickly into a rebellious sort of survival mode while Hook is forever haunted by how he might have succeeded.

Then, there are some whose formal education serves them well through their normal daily lives. The two characters who come most immediately to mind are Rat and Badger from *The Wind in the Willows*. Both of these characters show signs of educated intelligence, especially as we note Rat's enjoyment for writing poetry, but also as we note Badger's polished, formal language and manners. Both are legitimate peers of their more foppish friend, Toad, and yet both call upon their perspectives to identify his superficial and self-destructive behavior. I could add to this group the Weasley family, who appear to thrive as wizards and Hogwarts alumni, with neither the ego of a

Malfoy, the defensiveness of Hermione, nor the occasional resentment felt by Harry. For that matter, from Lewis' novel contrast Peter and Susan with Edmund, the latter of whom is openly acknowledged for having suffered in school, and who moves through most of the novel as if (Hook-like) he has been denied the best of what his older two siblings seem to take for granted, and Lucy (in her innocence) has not learned to miss.

Another common educational theme among these British children's classics is the prevalence of forces holding people back from the learning they are destined to achieve. Mole is one example; Bilbo Baggins is another. Mole's case differs, of course, from Bilbo's in that Mole does launch his own excursion. His rise from his mole hole comes after an expression of frustration at being stuck in his annual routine of spring cleaning, and his plight of nature to dwell underground. Mole leaves his humble abode to discover life in the larger world, but (as Bilbo might initially have predicted) Mole discovers an array of threats and eccentricities in the going out that make him wish he'd stayed in. By contrast, Bilbo's excursion is not initiated by his own volition. Like his hobbit neighbors in the Shire, he would be perfectly happy to live a quiet, peaceful life in his hobbit hole and never be drawn out into an adventure to slay a dragon and capture a magic ring. Yet, he is selected for just such an adventure, and in rising to that challenge he becomes more aware of the part of himself (the Tookish part) that ultimately isn't fully satisfied with a simple life. But whether called or driven, there are characters within this literary tradition whose education takes them out into a world that, no matter how promising, is much less comfortable than the one they occupied before their education begins.

Alice offers a variation of this image, though (like Mole) even in her story's beginning she is so done with her current world and ongoing education that she is nearly unconscious with boredom. The White Rabbit awakens a curiosity already desperate to be awakened. As a twist on this idea, Mr. Darling is also an example, far more intent at the beginning of Peter Pan to maintain the equilibrium of his proper British life than be shaken into an education that his adventurous children provide.

Yet another educational idea threaded through British Children's literature is a celebration of carefully scaffolded experiential learning. Alice, Mole, Bilbo and Harry Potter all highlight this value, but it is also championed in Beatrix Potter's tales and Lewis' novel. In Potter, the problems each animal faces bring with them threats of failure, but also means of resolution, as well as guardians nearby who themselves are masters of the relevant experience. The characters who seem not to learn their lessons are those who unreflectively escape experience (think, Jeremy Fisher) or whose ignorance seems its own reward (think, Tabitha Twitchett, and her hopeless mismanagement of her kitten, Tom). The characters who seem the best model of success are those who become small scale heroes because of simply plying their trade (think, Mrs. Tiggywinkle and John Joiner).

In *The Lion, the Witch, and the Wardrobe*, the old professor encourages Peter and Susan to use precedent and reason when evaluating Lucy's story of the wardrobe. His feedback helps them to sort through the integrity of their younger sister, and the corruption of their younger brother. Once they are, themselves, in Narnia, they bring that open mindedness to their personal encounters with Mr. Tumnus, the Beavers, and their redeemable brother, Edmund. Meanwhile, Edmund, from one perspective lacking in the proper scaffolding to understand the White Witch's tricks, falls for those tricks but remains open to one of the most important elements of experiential learning—a change of heart after experiencing the sacrifice of Aslan.

Which presents yet another key educational idea—that of the One Great Teacher. One consistent characteristic of those teachers is that people around them accept them as Great Teachers. McGonagall, Hagrid, even Snape recognize Dumbledore as the wise leader that he is. Likewise, Aslan's power and influence is unquestioned by Tumnus and The Beavers, but even the White Witch identifies him as the One to conquer in order to maintain her own power. Another characteristic of those Great ones is, so to speak, the size of their classes. Each of these teachers has primary influence over a small number of students, and in most cases only one particularly chosen student. Bilbo, Harry, Mole, they are all taken especially under the care respectively of Gandalf, Dumbledore, and Rat. Even with a somewhat larger "class," Aslan mainly speaks to the four children of the prophecy, the Daughters of Eve and Sons of Adam, and Mrs. Darling to her three children, especially Wendy.

Likewise, all of the Great Teachers are in one way or another unreachable in any long term or practical way. Gandalf comes and goes as his missions and sense of need demands, and always to the cause of leaving Bilbo the kind of space and opportunity to discover his own power. Aslan's very nature is illusive, gone during the White Witch's reign, returning when he senses the four children's presence in Narnia, and then leaving them in power following his relatively momentary intervention (via both ordinary magic, and deeper magic). Even Dumbledore, who is a daily presence at Hogwarts, conducts most of his "teaching" from a distance or in private, either by leaving material for Harry to explore on his own, or meeting with Harry in his chambers for sort of one on one tutorials reserved for the prize pupil. Peter stays in Neverland, as he hosts generations of Darling children who will pass through his domain and return to an adulthood empowered by imagination. And, from the other side of this narrative, Mrs. Darling does most of her important teaching before the story even begins, in all those quiet moments of tidying up her children's minds as they sleep. By the time they need her lessons, she has become a force they have within themselves while she, herself, remains in London (as will, in time, her daughter, Wendy), only hoping her lessons have taken hold. Even Rat, perhaps the most pedestrian of the Great Teachers, knows how to leave his student alone as that student becomes ready to learn, and he knows how to respond when that student needs to be rescued from the Wild Wood or indulged in a visit back to his humble home. Mole's final call to action sees his main teacher, Rat (being a poet), granted a position of understood aloofness, Rat's work with Mole now completed and the young charge quite able to apply the necessary practical and strategic skills to the battle for Toad Hall.

All of these teachers also call upon a source of power that is portrayed, in one way or another, as magic. While Gandalf and Dumbledore are both literally wizards, and Aslan is a giant, supernatural lion who serves allegorically as the son of God, even the Water Rat draws upon an unself-conscious confidence, a knowledge of the wide world, and an instinct about the wild woods and the river bank, a way even of preparing a picnic that to him seems ordinary and yet to his student is an absolute miracle. There are teachers like this in the world at large. They have charisma and brilliance, they garner the respect of their colleagues, and for the few select students whom they identify as ready, they are life-changers. However, most great teachers are especially effective because they primarily are good teachers, with reliable, adaptable methodology, tireless work ethic, effective interpersonal instincts, and their own evergrowing knowledge of themselves and the field in which they're teaching.

Such a teacher is Professor Lupin, and such a teacher is the Old Professor whose questions and listening patience help the Pevensie children to trust their sense and conscience. Such a teacher is Wendy, who learns from Peter Pan, and yet conveys her growing wisdom along to her "students," her brothers and the Lost Boys, through stories, role play, direct instruction (to help them remember their pasts), and modeling. Such a teacher is Alice, to and for herself, engaging in a novel-length experiment in trial and error, learning through action, observation, and language, the growing nuances of "who are you," where she wants to go, how to use the proper tools to get there, and how to hold her own once she has arrived. Once she has returned from those experiences, her first act is one of pedagogy, telling her sister all about her "dream," a bookend gesture to her sister's initial school book lessons that open the novel. Her second act is guidance, as (presumably later) she ushers Dinah through the Looking-Glass. Her third act is continuing education, as in that second novel individuals become communities and answers become ethics.

Consequently, the novels visited here celebrate diverse approaches to learning and learners and to children themselves, as valid and active learners even (especially) when left on their own in a stimulating, puzzling, or "curious" environment. These novels also celebrate imagination, carefully defined, as a learning tool. In *Peter Pan*, imagination at first seems to threaten the fragile stability of the Darling household. In Neverland, imagination alone seems unsatisfying in contrast with imagination in the service of role playing games or narrative. While Wendy seems to understand the importance of maintaining a clear distinction between the reality that she doesn't want to forget, and the imagination fueling enchanting games and stories, Peter's inability to make that distinction is presented as a flaw. His is an imagination that renders everything, even family, love, and food, into a game. Edmund falls prey to this particular corruption of imagination, mistaking (at first) Turkish Delight for substantive nourishment, while readers learn that the more of it he eats, the hungrier he becomes.

For Alice, imagination, an impulsive curiosity, a belief in something she had not yet experienced, is what leads her down the rabbit hole and through a series of learning stages. Characters that call upon her to trust her imagination present her with guidance and challenge, and leave her with an experience that she both identifies as a dream and retains as meaningful experience. Thus, by the end of *Through the Looking-Glass*, Alice not only shares her experience as if it were a dream, but claims that dream as her own and identifies herself as a dreamer. Imagination apart from reality does not by default become pure imagination, but rather it highlights (through both contrast and denial) the painful features of reality that imagination cannot remedy. These works of literature consistently promote healthy imagination as productive educational fuel, freeing the learner to make connections, pursue questions, and find joy well beyond the boundary of formal education. Contrarily, they caution readers that when imagination is used, not to engage in reality more playfully but rather to hide from it, the results include resentment, isolation, even insanity. People, characters, students who use imagination for protection or escape become, at best, narcissistic or silly like Tweedle-Dee and Tweedle-Dum or the Mad Hatter, and at worst as corrupted as Edmund or as evil as Quirrell, both of whom follow their imaginations into the service of an exploitive and abusive (not empowering, liberating) force.

So, I conclude with commentary about educational outcomes—to liberate or control, to empower or overpower, to bore with useless details or to inspire with curiosity and action? Seen as studies of education, the collection of British children's literary classics considered here consistently honors an individual's development of personal awareness and intellectual curiosity and power as the most important educational outcomes. Consequently, they also consistently identify the rote learning of fragmented information, especially for the purpose of recitation and assessment, not only as the educational outcome least useful to a well-educated adult life, but as a perennial obstacle to personal awareness and intellectual power. Formal education is the weeds and suckers in the garden of authentic learning, and this insight is offered by these nineteenth- and twentieth-century British writers, most of whom were closely associated with the most traditional educational systems on the planet. An education that controls and overpowers produces adults like Mr. Darling, Captain Hook, Professor Quirrell, the Dursley's, or Alice's sister with her book with no pictures or conversation, or Owl and Rabbit (innocently certain as they are in their misguided initiatives), or Eeyore and Tigger (each living in, and usually blinded by, the extremes of absolutism).

An education that liberates and empowers produces the kinds of adults that the Alice's, Wendy's, and Pooh's may grow into, pursuing their productive paths into the world, their ways well-lit and hearts well-illuminated by some extremely wise and loving teachers. It is an educational outcome that offers hope to the returning Lost Boys and even to Mr. Darling who appears to have learned from his earlier misplacement of priorities. It is an educational outcome that offers hope to Alice's sister who appears at the end of Carroll's first novel to have a change of heart as she listens to Alice's story. It offers hope to Alice, herself, ultimately through her best education having become the author of her own dreams. It is an educational outcome that offers hope to Christopher Robin as he leaves for the often rigid, even abusive structures of formal education after spending a portion of his childhood in the Hundred Acre Wood with a very good role model. It is an educational outcome that redeems Edmund and validates Lucy. It allows both Mole and Bilbo their adventures and transformations, while enriching their appreciation for themselves and their origins.

So, as I close these readings, what I hope I have argued well is that regardless of their authors' conscious intentions, these classics from British Children's Literature offer some very real and significant commentary on the enterprises of education. Whether your return to them has enriched your appreciation for the literature, or expanded your thinking about teaching and learning, or both, I invite you to continue looking for serious educational insights in the most unlikely and whimsical places—down a rabbit hole, through a wardrobe, beyond a train station platform, or in an enchanted corner of your own regularly tidied mind.

Bibliography

Anderson, Robert. "Elite Formation and Excellence in Modern Britain." *Annali della Scula Normale Superiore di Pisa. Classe di Lettere e Filosofia* 3, no.1 (2011), 71–80.

Barrie, J. M. *Peter Pan and Other Plays*. New York: Oxford University Press, 1995.

Barrie, J. M. *Peter Pan: Peter and Wendy, and Peter Pan in Kensington Gardens*. New York: Penguin Books, 2004.

Carroll, Lewis. *Alice's Adventures in Wonderland*. London: Puffin Books, 1994.

Carroll, Lewis. *Alice's Adventures in Wonderland and Through the Looking-Glass*. New York: Oxford University Press, 2009.

Dewey, John. *Democracy and Education*. New York: The Free Press, 1966.

Dickinson, Emily. *The Complete Poems of Emily Dickinson*. Boston: Little, Brown and Company, 1960.

Duckworth, Angela. *Grit: The Power of Passion and Perseverance*. New York: Charles Scribner's Sons, 2016.

Dweck, Carole. *Mindset: The New Psychology of Success*. New York: Ballantine Books, 2006.

Ericsson, Anders. *Peak: Secrets from the New Science of Expertise*. New York: Mariner Books, 2017.

Erikson, Erik. *Childhood and Society*. New York: W.W. Norton and Company, 1950.

Farenga, Pat. "About Growing Without Schooling." Accessed October 6, 2020. http//www.johnholtgws.com.

Gatto, John Taylor. *Dumbing Us Down: The Hidden Curriculum of Compulsory Schooling*. Gabriola Island, BC, Canada: New Society Publishers, 2005.

Goodlad, John I. *A Place Called School: Prospects for the Future*. New York: McGraw-Hill Book Company, 1984.

Gilligan, Carol. *In a Different Voice: Psychological Theory and Women's Development*. Cambridge, MA: Harvard University Press, 1982.

Goldstein, Dana. *The Teacher Wars: A History of America's Most Embattled Profession*. New York: Anchor Books, 2014.

Grahamme, Kenneth. *The Wind in the Willows*. London: Puffin Books, 1994.

Hillocks, Jr., George. *Research on Written Composition.* Urbana, IL: ERIC Clearinghouse on Reading and Communication Skills, 1986.

Hillocks, Jr., George. *Teaching Writing as Reflective Practice.* New York: Teachers College Press, 1995.

Hillocks, Jr., George. *Ways of Thinking, Ways of Teaching.* New York: Teachers College Press, 1999.

Hirsch, E. D. *Cultural Literacy: What Every American Needs to Know.* New York: Vintage Books, 1988.

Hirsch, E. D., ed. *What Your 6th Grader Needs to Know.* New York: Doubleday, 1993.

Holt, John. *How Children Learn* (Revised Edition). New York: Merloyd Lawrence, 1983.

Illich, Ivan. *Deschooling Society.* New York: Harper and Row, Publishers, 1970.

Jensen, George, and John K. DiTiberio. *Personality and the Teaching of Composition.* New York: Ablex Corporation, 1989.

Jung, Carl. *Memories, Dreams, Reflections.* New York: Vintage Books, 1989.

Kohlberg, Lawrence. *The Philosophy of Moral Development.* New York: Harper and Row, 1981.

Lewis, C. S. *The Lion, the Witch, and the Wardrobe.* New York: Harper Trophy, 1994.

Milne, A. A. *The World of Pooh: The Complete Winnie-the-Pooh and The House at Pooh Corner.* New York: E.P. Dutton & Company, Inc., 1957.

Montessori, Maria. *The Absorbent Mind.* New York: Holt, Rinehart, and Winston, 1967.

A Nation at Risk: The Imperative for Educational Reform. Washington, DC: U.S. Government Printing Office, April 1983.

Palmer, Parker. *The Courage to Teach.* San Francisco: Jossey-Bass, 2007.

Pearson, Carol. *The Hero Within: Six Archetypes We Live By.* New York: HarperOne, 1986.

Plato. *The Republic of Plato.* Translated by Allan Bloom. New York: Basic Books, 1968.

Potter, Beatrix. *The Complete Tales of Beatrix Potter.* London: Penguin Random House, Frederick Warne & Company, 1989.

Ravitch, Diane, and Chester Finn. *What Do Our 17-Year Olds Know?: A Report on the First National Assessment of History and Literature.* New York: HarperCollins, 1989.

Rousseau, Jean-Jacques. *Emile, or On Education.* Translated by Allan Bloom. New York: Basic Books, 1979.

Rowling, J. K. *Harry Potter and The Sorcerer's Stone.* New York: Scholastic, 1999.

Rowling, J. K. *Harry Potter and the Chamber of Secrets.* New York: Scholastic, 2000.

Rowling, J. K. *Harry Potter and the Prisoner of Azkaban.* New York: Scholastic, 2001.

Tolkien, J. R. R. *The Hobbit.* New York: Ballantine Books, 1982.

Vygotsky, Lev. *Thought and Language: Revised and Expanded Edition.* Cambridge: MIT Press, 2012.

Index

About the Author

For more than thirty years, **Thomas Albritton** has taught in the department of English and the Stout School of Education, as well as in the Global Studies and First Year Seminar programs at High Point University, North Carolina. His work focuses especially on children's and young adult literature, adolescent and adult literacy, and teacher imagery in popular culture.